MW01538784

The Musings of One

A - N - G - R - Y

Canadian Zebra

Kenneth J McKnight

◆ FriesenPress

Suite 300 - 990 Fort St
Victoria, BC, Canada, V8V 3K2
www.friesenpress.com

Copyright © 2015 by Kenneth J. Mcknight
First Edition — 2015

All rights reserved.

All rights reserved. No part of this publication may be reproduced, stored in a retrieval system or transmitted in any form or by any means - electronic, mechanical, photocopy, recording or any other - except for brief quotations in printed reviews, without the prior permission of the author.

ISBN
978-1-4602-7361-6 (Hardcover)
978-1-4602-7362-3 (Paperback)
978-1-4602-7363-0 (eBook)

1. History, Canada

Distributed to the trade by The Ingram Book Company

Front cover painting by artist Amanda MacLellan 2014 and used courtesy of the artist.

Preface

"Why", you may ask, "did you wait until you were over 75 years old before embarking on your autobiography?"

I guess I naively thought racial attitudes toward bi-racial / mulatto, ie: black and white, would have moderated and mellowed in this day and age, particularly in my beloved Canada. I was wrong.

Although some progressive souls embrace black and white relationships, many others probably don't realize the hurt and damage they do to innocent people with their negative attitudes.

By passing for white, I have been extremely vulnerable and have suffered much emotional hurt from these remarks. Decent, good people would never make racial remarks face-to-face to a black or mulatto person. Why do they feel it is acceptable in any circumstance? How do they know if everyone there is truly white? How would they feel to find out they've slandered one of the people in that cozy little conversational group? Sadly, they are racist without even knowing it. Think about it. It hurts.

My mission is to get the majority of people to search their souls. I will never change the 'sheet-wearing hard-core' racist. However, if more people become aware and responsible for their language, they will quit telling racial 'jokes' and stop the inuendoes. By reading my book, you just may become a better person. My mission will be accomplished.

I realized that as I was working with the publisher, that content editing was suggested. I appreciated the concept, but wanted to retain my own clear voice. Please excuse any brashness you may feel occurs.

It is also my hope that my grandchildren and family will better understand their family background and understand who I am, and how that has impacted their lives.

In addition, I wanted to celebrate the wonderful opportunities available to Canadians - namely that I was able to spend 20 years in our military learning highly technical occupations and then able to persist - be determined enough - to follow my dream of higher education and become a high school teacher, teaching electronics, for an additional 20 years. In hindsight, I had set my goals and acted on them over a number of years!

I hope that my story will inspire others to follow their dreams. A satisfying and fullfilling life is out there for everyone when they dream 'with action' and then move forward to achieve!

Acknowledgements

Many thanks to the following people to whom I owe so much in completing this project.

Alphabetically, they are:

Amanda MacLellan - My very talented illustrator for the front cover

Carol Ann Lease - My darling daughter who typed my
original manuscript - truly a labour of love

Code Workun - My Author Account Manager for FriesenPress - Publisher

Margaret McKnight - My diligent wife who confirmed
and corrected my memory of our 56 years together.
Thanks for your patience and support. I love you.

Sandra J Valks   CLU, DTM - 'Distinguished Toastmaster' - My
mentor - tormentor - editor - and damn good friend! :)

Table of Contents

Introduction

ZEBRA! ZEBRA! ZEBRA!

This is the name given to bi-racial folks - by a few nasty racists.

The first time I ever heard this outlandish metaphor was fifty years ago, when I was about twenty-five. The person, in question, wasn't referring to me, but rather to two young toddlers. Their father was a tall, and distinguished-looking black man, and their mother was a petite and blue-eyed blonde woman. She was white like my grandmother!

I was in Puerto Rico, one February, on an anti-submarine operation for a two-week period with the Royal Canadian Air Force. Some of our ground crew were enjoying a few beers on a beautiful beach. We were all gawking at the lovely young women in their scanty bathing suits. One Canadian Leading Aircraftman (LAC) quietly whispered, "Look at the Zebras!" He was referring to those little bi-racial toddlers with their blonde hair, and mocha-coloured skin. These were beautiful little children who were being "slurred" by some crude airman, who laughed, while others seemed very puzzled.

As for me, I was shocked, and for once in my life, I was speechless! The word 'Zebra' was emblazoned into my very being, like a song going around, and around, in my head, like a worm in my ear that I couldn't shake.

That was me. *Zebra, Zebra, Zebra*. I could hear it, over and over and over. Needless to say, I didn't like that tune. Believe me, being called a bi-racial sure beats being called a 'Zebra'!

I was eight-years-old when I first stumbled upon the fact that my grandfather was black. Before then, I had just thought of him as my grandfather. I only knew him for four years, from the ages of six to nine, at which point he passed away.

I never thought about his skin colour until the fateful day that my sister and I snooped through an old chocolate box full of memorabilia that we found in the closet. There, we found a gun licence for our Grandpa, Charles Wesley Webster. It listed his racial origin as "Negroid extraction." Since my discovery, I have chosen not to share this information with many people –only with a very few close acquaintances, and family. Some think I am undeservedly ashamed, while others think I'm oversensitive.

Quite frankly, Grandpa was Grandpa, and his colour was invisible. I simply grew up being 'me'.

I was not ashamed, nor proud, and I was not even aware that I was bi-racial.

Today, I think the reason for my anger, when I hear disparaging racial remarks about blacks, is that I reflect on the pain, the struggles, and upbringing that my mother experienced. Selfishly, deep down, I fear what would have happened to me had I displayed black traits. I wonder how I would have handled the struggles as a child, and a young adult. It scares me.

I often wonder whether it is fear that is the reason why some racist whites feel the need to slander blacks and bi-racials. Perhaps it's their own fear of losing their 'superiority.'

How many times have I personally been called 'Zebra'? Never – not even once – because I've never told anyone I am bi-racial. I don't look black; I look like a typical Anglo-Saxon Caucasian. When you look white, and travel in the white man's world, you surely get to hear a belly full of racial remarks, and innuendos. So keeping my bi-racial secret was painful.

It has been said, by smarter men than I, that, "Readers won't listen to the rants, ravings, and tirades of a totally angry man."

I concur, and couldn't agree more. So let me 'colour' my life story with humour and compassion. I promise to be very tolerant of some misinformed, racist, white folk. I promise that I will moderate my anger towards the mixed-up minority of racist whites in the writing of this exposé. My rage will be tempered by seventy-five-years of ups and downs, and by the fact that I have been moderately-successful, living in the white man's world. My perverse sense of humour aids, and abets, my outlook.

I also want my grown grandchildren to enjoy this book. They all have families of their own now, and are old enough to understand.

Yes, I do speak, and write, proper English. I credit this to the white man's education system. I may, sometimes, resort to jargon. This is how many white men perceive conversation between black people. Yes, I am angry, but I will temper that anger to show you how ludicrous the beliefs of the white racists were, and probably, still are.

The shaping of this racially-troubled man stems from this racially-troubled land. Where else are immigrants welcomed so openly? Yet people who have been here for generations are spurned, scorned, and segregated only because of their colour. Guess what y'all? It ain't the good ole U.S. of A. It's Canada, eh. Canuck! Yes – this sick, prejudiced, country is Canada. Our aboriginals have been put upon for generations. And black people have barely been tolerated because they are so few in number.

The black race has been subjected to persecution, and belittlement. You can, if you want, believe general statements from the United Nations. The U.N. says Canada is a great place to live. My quote continues: "AS LONG AS YOU ARE WHITE." End of quote.

Yes, I am a Zebra. I am not proud of it. I am not ashamed of it. This fact is completely out of my hands.

I remember learning from old movies, and tough pocket novels, that it would be a foolish white man who would confront a black man one-on -one. The stereotype of a black man is a man with a razor in his shoe, a pig-sticker in his pocket, and a Saturday night special on his hip. Oh yes! How I learned from the movies!

"When Whitey gets together with his redneck buddies, the gloves are off. The hate and derision just pours from their brown, and crooked, teeth. Black is bad. Bad is black."

I would wake up in nightmarish sweats, hearing, and seeing, these unsavoury visions. These apparitions seemed ingrained into my very being. Oh God, I thought, I was getting as bad as the white racists!

An automatic reset had to go off in my head if I were to learn to cope. It did!

When you pass as white, as I did, you sure got an earful of prejudice. I came to understand why some blacks refer to the white man as "Whitey" or "Redneck." I don't condone their words, but I understand the frustration, and the need to fight back.

If you didn't have a sense of humour, and some self-confidence, the racial verbal diarrhea could destroy you. Many Zebras have been shaken to the core. Not me! Let's get started!

Chapter One

It All Started with Grandpa Charlie

My grandfather, Charlie Wesley Webster, was a black man from Missouri. (Black is in – Negro is out -- don't y'all know dat?) His father had been a freed slave. Grandpa Charlie had just missed official slavery at the end of the American Civil War. Although he missed the official humiliation, and degradation, the real hatred was still there.

Charlie headed for Alberta, which was then part of the Northwest Territories of Canada (N.W.T.). Alberta became a province in 1905.

He had decided to head for the land of the free. What a joke on him. He lived, primitively, east of Calgary. He must have snickered at his aristocratic name.

Grandpa Charlie trained rich professionals' purebred dogs. He also collected junked farm wagons, and later on, junked cars. It was still junk.

He became very lonely in his isolated world.

Charlie married by Grandmother, Marie, who was white, and from England. Back then, mixed marriages between whites and black/ Negroes were unheard of. When we were kids, we heard stories that these marriages were trouble; they could get your house burned down with you, and your family in it, in our version of the Wild West. Folklore, or fact? I'm not sure, but society frowned on mixed marriages, especially when the male was black.

Jolly Old England had its own way of thinking. They thought they had a surplus of lower class females to dole out. At first, England's plan sounded benevolent. It would reduce the number of female bond servants available for the upper class. The British would supply steerage class passage on a ship for the young damsels. A pre-arranged marriage would take place after the couple physically met. The only qualification for the suitor was that he had to have, at least, a modest means of income, and probably some land. Charles Wesley Webster had the name, and very little else.

What was a vulnerable, penniless, English lass supposed to do? The voyage from England, to Halifax, plus the train ride to Calgary, was extremely trying, and fatiguing. The Canadian Pacific Railway (C.P.R.) had cut rates for immigrants, and labourers heading for Alberta, and the Northwest Territories. It was still the Wild, Wild West for many years to come.

Marie had never seen a black man in her life. Nothing had prepared her for the sight of him. It was never mentioned that he was black or Negroid, in any correspondence. Marie decided to make the best of a desperate situation. The fair-skinned, blue-eyed blonde was more than Charlie ever could have dreamed of. He worshiped her.

Their union resulted in two offspring: my mother Dorothy Marie and my Uncle Harry. Dot, as my mother was called, was a slim beauty, with foxy curves. She had mostly English, and Caucasian, features. Her thin British nose, and red lips, belied her heritage. Her flashing black eyes set off her black wavy hair. Her hair bordered on kinky. If you knew her lineage, then you could see that her Negroid traits stood out. Uncle Harry had hazel eyes, wavy brown hair, and a gift of the gab. He had an eye for beautiful women, and collected a bit of a harem. He used to brag, "What they say about black men is true." Harry had no obvious traces of being part black but he often pointed out that he never had any complaints from his women.

Unfortunately, for my mother, and Uncle Harry, their mother didn't stick around. She flew the coop. Who could blame Grandmother Marie for leaving, considering the poverty she experienced after she had tried to escape the same in England. Five thousand miles later, she still had to deal with coal oil lamps, outhouses, and abject poverty. Marie abandoned her children, and her husband. Poor Grandma had vanished and remained untraceable for many years.

My father Bud came into this racially-mixed potpourri. Dorothy Marie set her sights on him. He had immigrated to Canada, when he was four years old, riding his horse to the Alberta border. The horse was more afraid of him than he was afraid of the horse. My Dad was a mean little boy with alabaster skin, blue eyes, and black hair. He was a racist, and mean, for as long as I can remember. Ironic, isn't it? Bud didn't like blacks but ended up marrying my bi-racial mother?

My Grandfather, Charles Wesley, didn't take it well that my mom was going to marry "white trash". He was deadly with a shotgun, and by the time Bud came along, he had had his fill of Whitey. First, there was segregation, then racial intolerance, and the final straw was his wife leaving him for "white trash." No "white trash" was going to marry his daughter.

That's why Ma and Pa eloped, and disappeared into the wild mountains of western Alberta. Ironically, my sister Gayle's birthplace is called Whitecourt, Alberta.

Gayle always was a bit darker than I was. If visions of Nelson Eddy, Rose Marie, and a rustic cabin fill your thoughts, think again. We lived in a barn board shack. The relatives had to keep gloves on when playing cards to keep their hands warm. My aunt told that story many, many times.

Years later, Gayle's heritage came back to haunt her. Her first husband's Yankee relative took one look at her and said, "You are not a bad cook for an Indian." Gayle cried for a week over this jerk's remarks.

Barn board shack where my sister Gayle was born 1938.
Located in Whitecourt, Alberta. It was so cold, our
parents had to wear gloves when playing cards!

Ken with sister Gayle in 1942 – War Years in New Brunswick – Where we toasted bread over the wood stove grates because of black-out orders.

Ken and Gayle in 1946 in best school togs living at Singh's Cabins, Calgary

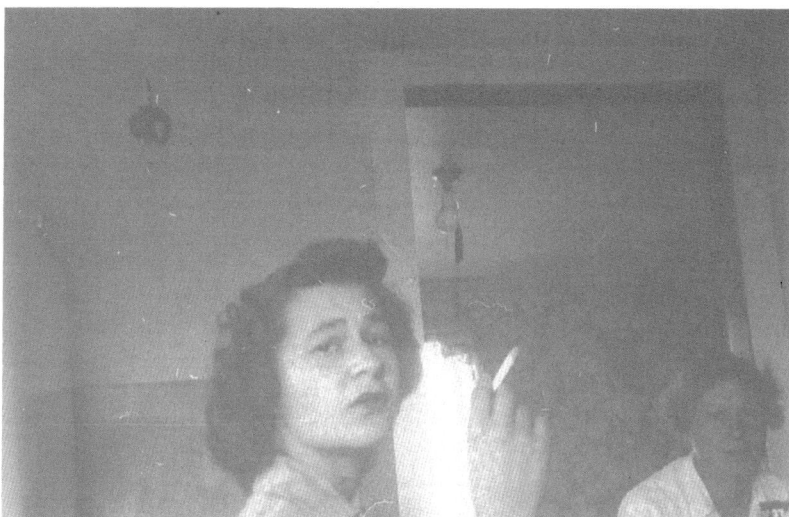

Gayle and Mom. In later years, Gayle was told, "You're not a bad cook for an Indian." Gayle cried for a week over this jerk's remarks.

Chapter Two

Ma and Pa and My Early Years

My aunts filled me in on Dot and Bud's tumultuous union. Domestic bliss, it wasn't. Ma had a wacky sense of humour. She had said they named Labour Day for her. After all, that was when she went into labour with me. She also blamed me for WWII. The War started on the 3ʳᵈ of September, 1939. She got all upset and excited, and delivered me on the 4ᵗʰ of September, 1939. That's when I poked my head out into this world. Many a time, afterward, I wanted to pull it back in!

I have no recollection of my early childhood, so dad's sisters, in later years, helped piece it together.. My aunts weren't overly fond of my mulatto mother. Dad was the baby of the family of six, or seven; the exact number is unknown to me. My aunts always spoiled him, and put up with Ma for dad's sake. However, they were totally supportive of us two kids. I don't think we could have survived without our aunts' help and support.

Poverty drove Dad to Edmonton. Besides, he was happy to be two hundred miles from Grandpa Charlie's shotgun. He got a job flooding outdoor skating rinks for a few cents per hour. Two thugs chased him three miles for the seventy-five cents he hid in his dungarees. They didn't get it. Like I said, he was one tough son of a gun!

Dad joined the patriotic flood of volunteers who joined the army for a steady job. The depression created many patriotic, paid soldiers. Even so, they were all more patriotic than many rich, farmers' sons who stayed home with an, "Essential Personnel Freeze" designation. They weren't going to get their tails shot off.

My good-looking, smooth talking, Uncle Harry was a woman-izer. So he was happy to receive the exempt status. There was a real shortage of men on the home front. This rogue tried to fill the void single-handedly! His "Essential Service" designation was to help the war effort; it wasn't for servicing beautiful women, but he was happy to be of service. For his day job, Uncle Harry worked in a munitions factory. Our family was transferred to Nova Scotia. My first recollections were of war-time blackouts. No lights were allowed to show. Windows were draped in black, and lights were kept low. We used to toast bread on the grates of a wood stove where all we could see were the embers.

My dad's friend, Gord, flooded the community's large ice rink, and one time, all hell broke loose. Some black soldiers from Africville stole a Jeep, and rutted our freshly-flooded community ice rink. Cursing and shouting rang out. I didn't understand the words, but the anger and cursing were intense. Words like, "burr-head, black bastard, and oh yes, nigger", filled the air. If the locals would have caught those soldiers, I'm sure 'southern justice', the rope, would have prevailed.

Nova Scotia has not been very tolerant when it comes to black people. A black couldn't be buried in a white man's cemetery until the mid-1960s. Look it up in the historical newspapers if you find this hard to believe.

Africville was the black suburb of Halifax. It had very few amenities compared to those received by other suburban communities. Africville was later bulldozed on the pretext that a bridge right of-way was needed. Little, if any, of the promised compensation was paid. Shame on the few bigoted, arrogant leaders who made such a decision!

Before dad left for overseas, Ma and Pa used to take us for walks. I was very small with short legs. Pa set a really fast pace so that I couldn't keep up, and I was totally frustrated. I finally let him have it!

"You doordy Bastoids make me walk so fast I have to wun," I shouted. They both laughed at me. We were a very irreverent family.

My speech impediment disappeared when I was ten-years-old. (More on that later.)

Aside from having my foot gashed by a large, tin can lid, (I still have the scar), life was good for this four-year-old. The train trip to Calgary would soon shatter my idyllic Eastern life.

"Penguins, Mom, look penguins," I shouted, excitedly. They weren't penguins at all; they were a gaggle of Roman Catholic nuns. Did I get my butt warmed for that one! The nuns were nice to us, and fed us candy.

Things went downhill from there. The train stopped at a station, and I got off. The fellow driving the baggage tractor thought I was a local, and let me ride on the tractor. The train started to pull out, and then came to a sudden stop. Ma sailed down the steps, covered in soap lather, wearing just her slip. She had been taking a sponge bath when she spotted me, just as the train was pulling out. She was madder than a wet hen. I behaved for the rest of our trip.

Our new home was called "Singh's Cabins"; it was located on the MacLeod Trail, just south of Calgary. The places were dumps, with outside toilets, and an outside community hand pump for your water.

It was so cold, when the coal fire went out in the winter, the goldfish bowl froze. We kids thought the fish were dead so we threw them on the roof, and watched them slither down the roof slope. It seems I had an attitude even back then.

As kids, we were amazed by big trucks. One night, after the U.S. instituted a truck ban because of spring thaw, we had bumper-to-bumper trucks in the long driveway at Singh's Cabins. (All the kids thought it was a 'Road Band' not 'Road Ban'!) Every truck had its pretty clearance lights on. It was quite the spectacle for little kids but the trucks all cleared out in the morning, as soon as the road ban was lifted.

Grandpa Charlie was never afraid to defend hearth, and home, with his twelve gauge shotgun. We kept a few rabbits as pets, and one time, Charlie caught a weasel, who had decided to grab the rabbits by their throats, and eat them as his main course.

My grandfather had other ideas. When the weasel climbed a fence post, defiant and mean, Charlie let him have it with both barrels of his twelve gauge shotgun. The force knocked Charlie backwards, but the weasel looked like Swiss cheese. Meanwhile, Uncle Harry got upset, when he examined the shredded and ventilated pelt. It could have been worth a few bucks! But after Charlie got through with it, it was worth zilch.

I was so excited when it was time to enroll in school in early September. My birthday was September 4th, and I was now six. After two days of school, I thought I should move up to Grade Two because of my birthday. After a period of crying, and putting forth unconvincing arguments, I stayed in Grade One for the whole year. I wasn't special after all, and I still had my speech impediment, and attitude.

Chapter Three

My Formative Years - albeit My Misadventures

It was an understatement to say that my father, and I, didn't get along, so imagine my surprise when he sat me on his knee one day. We were surrounded by his cronies, all barely literate. He told them I would read to them out of my reader. The story was about *Nell the Horse.*

The text read, "Nell went trot, trot, trot down the road."

I started, "Nell went twat, twat, twat, down the woad."

They killed themselves laughing and told me that I was a great reader. They slapped me on the back.

"Read it again Kenny."

I had arrived! Dad's friends liked me, or so I thought.

"Nell went twat, twat, twat, down the woad," I repeated.

What a bunch a crap! I was about thirteen-years-old when I wised up to their street language.

We learned to smoke, swear and annoy, at an early age. We walked the highway, and picked up cigarette butts. We knew all about hygiene, so we cleverly broke the butts apart, and salvaged the unused tobacco. There were no restrictions those days on who could buy cigarette papers. We used new cigarette papers, rolled our lucifers, with the dirty tobacco, and we had a sanitary smoke. In retrospect, I can still see some rubby-dub drooling over his ciggy-butt before he threw it away for our consumption. Now, it makes my skin crawl.

I had one more lesson on smoking rehabilitation. Leonard, a big German kid, taught me how to roll a sanitary cigarette. We stole his mother's can of tobacco, and papers. His old lady caught us red-handed.

Of course, it was my fault! Geez, I was getting a complex. She sent her son outside, and it was just me, and the beast. The dragon-lady informed me I would not leave her custody until I smoked the whole can of tobacco. I thought she was trying to asphyxiate me with tobacco smoke. I threw the tobacco can at her head, and she ducked out of the line of fire. I made a bee-line for the door. Wow! My great escape. That broke my smoking habit for a long time. To hell with Nicorets! ™

Mrs. Wannamaker was one tough old teacher who worked out of our two-room schoolhouse, Glenmore School. She was straight from the ranch, and all the kids thought she was great. She showed us her saddle, her lariat, and spurs. On some occasions, she would wear her leather riding skirt. We were impressed.

She was teaching us about the fur trade, and how to tan skins and hides. She told the older boys to trap a gopher, a Richardson Ground Squirrel, to be precise. They had no luck, so she took gallons of water, poured it down a hole, where a gopher had disappeared, and waited. He came up p.d.q. (pretty darn quick). She brained him with a baseball bat, and took him to our classroom. She skinned him, and stretched his hide on a drying board. Then our teacher "tanned" his hide.

After a few days, she had a finished product and presented a Grade Four boy with the trophy. We were relieved, as most of us didn't want it, but we tried to act disappointed when we didn't win the tanned Richardson Ground Squirrel. The girls all freaked out, and ran scream-ing, and gagging, to the girls' cloakroom. All of us macho boys tried not to throw up and act tough, our version of tough, anyway.

Mrs. Wannamaker was only allowed to supply teach after that.

Because I was small, I got bullied constantly. One punk used to pound on me, randomly. That was, until my cousins took me to their farm, and pumped me up with hard work, and good food. By then, I had had a growth spurt that made me stronger, and taller. I was already mean.

The next school year, I waited for that punk, and shellacked him every day. An old guy witnessed one incident, and tried to intervene. I told him I had to beat this kid up because I was afraid he would pound me again. He laughed, and assured me this wouldn't happen. This punk and I co-existed until I left the neighbourhood.

It's a fact that girls mature earlier than boys. So one day, an older girl decided to take my friend, and me, on a little adventure. The only reason we went along with it was because we knew it was wrong. If it was wrong, we reasoned, it must be fun. We were nine-years-old and didn't have a clue, or the desire, to follow through.

Let's leave it at this: She wanted to play doctor but she couldn't go through with it, either. So the "doctor" cried, and ran home to her father. We were terrified and stayed out of his way. I saw her years later, at the Calgary Stampede. I was in their force, and she had matured into a striking young woman. Poor Beth got red, and looked at her feet. I must admit I wasn't much more composed than she was.

That same year, I was sure that I was getting a wagon for my birthday. Instead I got squat! Still smarting, I borrowed another kid's wagon. I put my right knee in the wagon and let my left leg pump, and kick, down the MacLeod Trail.

Although the highway terminated at the Montana border, it wasn't particularly busy. I went miles, and got over my disappointment about my birthday wagon. After I cooled off, I started the return journey. I was tired and worn to a frazzle. That's when I spotted this long hill, jumped in the wagon, and coasted at a good clip. I was going like stink, when I lost control and found myself airborne. I managed to sail across a deep, wide ditch --almost

Crash! The wagon was splintered, and I was bruised, and shaken. I had to pull the wrecked, splintered, wagon all the way home. The wagon wasn't the only thing that was beaten up that night. Although I had virtually no parenting, and no supervision, I learned one fact that day: Borrowing without permission is called stealing. I got waltzed around the woodshed plenty for that error in judgment.

"STEALING IS NOT GOOD." - especially if you got caught!

We were crazy about movies. I used to think, if I walked very slowly, under the marquee, my folks would magically take us to see a show. No such luck except once on my birthday. I was given a choice. I could go with Ma, and Gayle, to the Model "T" races, or go to a movie. I opted for the movie. Big mistake.

My babysitter was a teenager, who was star-struck, and an airhead. She took me to this tear-jerking, romantic, dewy-eyed love story. She cried all the way through it. I almost cried myself, but for different reasons. I could have been watching <u>real</u> races and <u>real</u> crashes.

I went to the washroom, and got lost. She didn't miss me until the movie was over. Meantime, Ma, and Gayle, got to ride back and forth in a taxi with Dad's friend, the Scalawag Gord who drove for United Cab, and was never far away. Me, I got to take a streetcar, and take a long, long walk home. Happy Birthday, Zebra.

Not long after the *Nell the Horse* debacle, another calamity hit. Pa had returned from the war, with a German belt, with a Swastika emblazed on it. I showed it off, and promptly lost it. He was not amused!

We were living hand-to-mouth but my folks always managed to have, and attend, house parties. To hell with school clothes! (It didn't matter: we kids were all in the same boat which made living in the poor house easier to accept.)

At one such gathering, Pa decided to play the fiddle. He started to play, and suddenly went white, and looked dumb-founded. It was one of the few times I felt sorry for him. He had lost part of his forefinger during the war. That night, all his hate for the Germans rose to the top, and spilled over. His language was as colourful, and racist toward the 'Krauts' (his word), as any white man could have directed towards blacks, and Zebras. I think he hated everyone.

Billy was an older kid, who had a job driving a horse, and a stone boat, which was a kind of a horse-drawn, large wheel barrow, with no wheels. The showboat slid on the snow. Billy hauled chopped grain in it.

He often let me tag along, and introduced me to a little B. and E. (Break and Enter). We would "jimmy" the door to the hired man's quarters, and devour his home-made cookies. The man either never caught on, or ignored it, as we didn't hurt his place at all. Eureka! No police record, yet, and I was almost in my pre-teen years.

Gayle and I went to different schools. Hers was very close to Calgary's city limits; mine was out in the sticks. Hers had outdoor toilets; mine were inside. Go figure!

After school, I would take waxed paper, and feed it to the goats that were fenced in along the way. I think they liked it. Tin cans were another matter. They would chew on the flattened cans but we knew they didn't swallow them. Our rationale? We never saw goat milk in a tin can! We thought it was a real funny joke.

There was a large tree, which was adjacent to another fenced field that had a long branch which protruded into a field full of bulls. I liked to climb, shimmy, and perch on the limb overlooking the bulls. I proceeded to wave a red jacket, and whistle at them. I was just getting their attention when – CRACK! The branch let go. I found myself flat on my back with the air knocked out of me. I also managed to get the bulls' attention.

When I looked up they were in a semi-circle around me. They say that fear conquers all. I managed to dig my heels in, and push myself, crab-like, under the barbwire to safety. After that incident, I related the tale of my heroic escape, and blustered about my bravery. Then, I found out the truth. They weren't bulls at all. They were just friendly milk cows satisfying their curiosity. My ego took another direct hit.

Some do-gooder thought "poor folk" should have limited, free, dental care. Damn right, limited. They would not pay for 'freezing' or 'gas', just drilling and filling. I found this out the hard way. It was after my "doctor" experience, at a time when I was developing an interest in girls. To show this skinny, young thing I was interested, and available, I used the caveman approach, and chased her. She feigned a 'hard-target' approach, and ran. She stopped suddenly for me to catch her. Trophy time!

I tripped and hit her skinny backbone with my jaw. I broke off one of my front teeth. Wow! The air passing over it hurt like the devil. The do-gooder dentist said, "Sorry that is cosmetic, so I have to charge." Guess what! I'm now seventy-five years old, and still have my broken tooth.

We were enchanted with our landlords at the cabins. They had bright turbans, and a pile of money. We thought they were all Rajas, like in the movies. Do you remember the Kaiser-Frazer Motor Car Company? One son had a new Kaiser, or Frazer, I'm not sure. He had lots of money and little practical experience. On more than one occasion, we saw it steaming, or smoking, in the long driveway. No sympathy from us.

At one point, we found ourselves moving! It was about time we started living the good life, I thought. Not so fast. We graduated from being poor to being really poor. (Poor Zebra.) Yes, we moved to Dog Patch.

Chapter Four

*New 'Shacky' House - New 'Shacky'
Neighbourhood - aka 'Dogpatch'*

Grandpa Charlie decided to move closer to Calgary, and he purchased two lots for fifteen dollars each. He built a shack in a largely unpopulated neighbourhood. Then his health failed, and the lots became my Ma's property. Harry, her brother, was cut out completely, although there wasn't much to be cut out of.

Dad borrowed four hundred dollars from his rich sister (rich by our standards). She drove Gayle, and me, to the farm most years but this time, she couldn't stop beefing, "What is he doing with the money?"

He was building a house, you old shrew!!! It was a 2-by-24 foot box with no bathroom, no water or electricity. The next year, we did get power. Wow! Progress! The house had a dug-out for a basement (cellar). There were three bedrooms that were 8-by-2 feet. We used blankets as doors. A lot of sex education took place here.

While our house was being built, we continued to live at Singh's Cabins. Gord, the Scalawag, drove us to our new school. (Gord was always in our life.) Mom, and Gord, dropped us off at this city school, King Edward, which was a towering sandstone building that looked like a fortress to a couple of ten- and eleven-year-olds. We were terrified.

When I say that we were dropped off, I meant really dropped off.

Ma didn't even come in to register us – she didn't help us at all..

School registration was an ordeal. "What nationality are you?" I kept answering 'Canadian' until they gave up. They finally decided we must be Scottish because of our name. I couldn't tell them I was American Negro, or Zebra, because I hadn't discovered it yet.

Gayle, and I, cowered on one side of the building. That's when the bullying started. We got dropped off on the boys' side. Gayle had to then go to the far girls' side. I thought I would never see her again. Somehow we found each other after school. It's a good thing we did because we had no idea how to get home. Some parents need a good kick-- white, black or Zebra!

Fortunately, we recognized some of the kids who lived in our shack town and they showed us how to get home. Ma, and the Scalawag, meanwhile, continued to build the house while Dad worked.

Our neighbourhood was nicknamed 'Dogpatch'. The locals, and those living in the surrounding area, knew the name well. It looked like it was out of the Ozarks. Most everyone had a dog to prevent gas theft because gas, at the time, was probably thirty-nine cents a gallon. Not a litre!

We raised rabbits for meat. We had large pen, on rollers, that could accommodate about thirty rabbits. After they finished grazing, through a chicken wire bottom, the whole pen was rolled a few feet to a new area. I named the rabbits after hockey players. The Calgary Stampeders played for the Allan Cup. Red Hunter, and Art Michaluk, were good players, and my favourite rabbits.

Pa forbade us from listening to the National Hockey League. His excuse? They were Eastern bastards! Strangely, when I came home from school one day, I saw the rabbit version of Michaluk hanging by his ears. Pa said he butchered him by mistake. After sixty-five years, I guess it is time to give him the benefit of the doubt.

Pa, and good ole Gord, used to poach game by shooting a 22. calibre rifle at ducks. They were very resourceful. It was totally illegal, prob- ably out of season, but the 22. calibre didn't make as much racket as a shotgun. (Maybe dad was still allergic to shotguns.)

Gord had been a game warden, and knew how not to get caught. They used to net whitefish at MacGregor Lake. While they fished, Gayle, and I, filled the whole car with tin cans full of sand to make a sandbox at home. The guys had a car full of white fish. Since the old car had no get up and go, our cans of sand got unloaded in a hurry.

Rich Aunt Sanny would trek to the States each fall. She had this huge, long, black Chrysler product which was pretty swanky for Dogpatch. She would sometimes give us an American silver dollar. (These large silver dollars were used a lot in Montana.) I remember listening to her car radio when Prime Minister McKenzie King died. I asked her what would happen to his Queen. She called me a dumb 'tar' baby.

I didn't know why, but dad tried to beautify our house. We could get lilac, and honeysuckle bushes, for nothing if we moved them from Mount Royal, a ritzy neighbourhood. The old man was in his glory.

I sure found out what hard work was. He borrowed a horse, and a dirt moving slip. The only problem was, he had a non-farmer for a son. Dad yelled, screamed, and swatted me, but he was nice to the horse. The horse got nervous, and stepped on my instep. I thought he had broken my foot. I think that's the only time the old man smiled all day. I sure was no cowboy.

We had a huge garden and it was my job to hoe it, while the other kids played scrub baseball. We just called it scrub. What to do? I cut the blooms off the spud plants with a hoe. I got my rear kicked, but it gave me some time to play ball. It was a compromise under duress.

Winters were better. We skated and played hockey well after dark. If we did our chores, loading wood and coal, and packing water, we were pretty well ignored.

Our schooling proved to be a problem. Gayle solved hers; she quit and got married really young. I was academically-gifted, and decided to give education a good go. We paid no city taxes, and there were no schools for miles in the country.

We were pawns to a bunch of mean-spirited bureaucrats so we were moved around a lot. It went like this: Grade Four (Glenmore); Grade Five (King Edward); Grade Six (Richmond); Grade Seven (King Edward); Grade Eight (Currie); Grade Nine (King Edward); and Grade 10 (Western Canada High School). It took a few months to realize we were "persona non-grata".

Every year, they would find us, and ban us from returning. At good old King Edward, they weren't very smart, and I was able to return every second year. Of course, those were the days before computers. My odyssey from one school, to another, lasted from 1949 to 1955. I felt like a bleeding ping-pong ball.

Mr. Callbeck was my first male teacher. He was my Grade Six teacher, at Richmond School. He was a prince. His understanding of troubled, and neglected, youth was uncanny. He was the genuine article. However, one day he came storming into class. This was totally out of character. He raised hell with us, and left the room. We were devastated. He was like all the people in Dogpatch. But he wasn't, of course. He quietly entered the room, and apologized to us kids. We found out he had just got word his daughter was terminally ill. God, we loved him.

Our Richmond soccer team had to play good old King Edward, my alma mater. Four of us piled onto this double-barred balloon tire bike, and headed into enemy territory. It wasn't long before the King Edward teachers yelled at us to stop and get off. We told them to 'flock' off, gave them the finger, and kept on going.

Bruce, Janet and I, always competed for top marks. The reward for the top student was that he or she would become the school patrol 'Captain' who wore a blue badge while the other patrollers got plain ones. In reality, we were just student crossing guards. But we thought we were hot stuff. We timed the safe crossing of students to the city bus schedule. It was a lot of responsibility for a little kid with a harness, white Sam Brown belt, and a sign to stop a large city bus. What a rush – temporary, of course -- as the bus drivers just blew the whistle on us. We barely kept our prestigious position of authority.

Dad had a Canadian Pacific Railway pass. The pass was good on both carriers. (Via was unheard of at that time.) The first time we used it was a disaster. He dropped us at the Canadian National Railway Station, and went to work. Guess what! No train. No phone, either. We were scared because the train ran only every second day. Luckily, we knew a woman, who lived a few blocks from the train station, who made a phone call to one of our neighbours. It was a long wait to be picked up after dad came home from work. He made no apologies or admissions of negative parental practices which was typical of parents in Dogpatch.

My folks must have paid taxes to some municipality somewhere. As you know, taxes are based on your property value, and ours was basically zilch. I think the municipality should have owed all of the Dogpatchers' money instead of vis-a-versa.

We had a couple of "half-houses" in our neighbourhood which were made from used and scrapped 2-by-4s that were laid flat, and nailed, one on top of the other, all the way up. This left the builder with 4-inch thick walls, in 2-inch increments all the way up to the roof. Each structure was then adorned with one half of a gable roof.

The intention was to leave the other side of the house, and the roof, to be completed later. It never happened. These half-houses survived long after I left Dogpatch.

A second housing style included the basement house. The builder would put heavy roofing on the top which was intended to be the future main floor, and then knock a doorway through the cement. But they would never ever finish them. That's because a fully-built house would mean a rise in the taxes to be paid.

The third housing style of choice was the streetcar model, and it was unique. Builders would strip the running gear, wheels, and every other part from underneath the streetcar, and then plunk them down on the ground with a hoist.

The final housing model, the 'piece de resistance', was the flat roof Dogpatch Model. The builder still used the stacked, nailed, 2-by-4 scrap wood, plunked a flat roof on it, and then layered the roof with tar paper, and rolls of roofing material.

Let's just say the homes in Dogpatch never won a "Better Homes and Gardens" awards.

Our neighbor, Alfy, and his family, lived in one of the old narrow streetcars. Poor Alfy. His kids had pet rabbits. We would let them out, and then we would catch them for him. He thought we were public-spirited young men. He would give us a small cash reward. I chased a rabbit under a stationery bulldozer once, and my head made contact with it. The dozer didn't move. Wow! What a headache. I guess I deserved that.

We used to take a few pop bottles from the back storage area of a small convenience store, and sell them back to the store-owner at the front. Between the rabbits, and the pop bottles, we had our version of what Ontarians call the 'In and Out' Beer Store.

I had a great year at Richmond School. However, as before, I was sent back to King Edward. During my Grade Seven, I saw a lot a bullying; it was not a stellar year.

I was caught, again, trying to go to the same school for two years in a row. In Grade Eight, I was shipped off to a new school, the Currie School, which was supposed to be a school for children whose parents were currently in the armed forces. Damn bureaucrats said we should go there because it was closer.

There was a downside to this placement -- having to wear the clothes. The armed forces' dependents were dressed to the nines, by our standards. I didn't have any decent clothes. My old man was a clean freak, on a frugal budget. I used to get my so-called clothes at 'Briggs Rags'. Most of their stuff was pretty bad, only good for wiper commercial rags. You might say they were grim pickings.

The place was so terrible that when we started sorting through the piles of real tired clothes, Pa came upon this big pile of cat feces. We were out of there in a hurry! I graduated to war surplus clothing. Pretty drab, but less breezy, and smelly.

Chapter Five

My Railway Pass - My Pass to Freedom

Dad's railway pass was my escape to sanity. I got to stay with big Aunt Frances who was married to a little shrimp called Herman. They reminded me of Mutt and Jeff. We used to call Herman 'Her Man'. Poor Uncle Herman had a stroke, and lost his speech, completely. He finally got frustrated. He tried so hard to say "Bullshit" so often, he finally said it. Bullshit was the only word he could say until his dying day. My Aunt Frances, who was called Aunt Frant, looked after him really well. So well, she would rack up bills, all over British Columbia, and start over in a new town. I got to see much of British Columbia that way.

The Alberta farm provided us with the opportunity to engage in a little "pig-riding". The pigs would head to the sty, their little pig house which looked more like a doghouse, and brush off the rider into the muck and crud. When this happened, the rider didn't smell too good, I'll tell you. We also liked to ride the steer. One time, this landed me in the hospital. That's my take on it, anyway. The steer bucked me off, and trampled me, on my side.

After getting home I was rushed to the hospital where I had my appendix removed p.d.q. - pretty darn quick.

I think I wore out my welcome, on the farm, after the barn roof painting fiasco. I was handing a bucket of green shingle paint up to my sister, Gayle, whom I had coaxed onto the roof. She was terrified of heights, and she dumped the whole shebang on me. I was a little green man. Whatever they used for paint remover stung like hell.

Before I left Currie School, we got even with the well-dressed dudes. My friend, Buddy, borrowed a horse. We rode it to school and rode it onto the soccer field. That was the first and only time, those kids felt envious towards me. I knew "envy" very well, and survived.

My fathers' lack of carpenter skills was well known. He got some help from the Scalawag Gord, and finished his dream project. It was a deluxe, two-holer, outside toilet with a window placed really high up. It was going to be a work of art, complete with wallpaper.

I was terrified when I found out I had to work with my Pa. He screamed, and hollered, and got my arm in a pincer movement. It hurt. I panicked, jumped off the toilet bench where I was standing, and landed in a huge open container of wallpaper paste. My interior design career was over. He completed it without me.

Pa stocked the two-holer with real toilet paper - not an Eaton's Catalogue. The day before the official christening, he picked up Gayle, and me, at the White Rose Service Station. That saved us walking twenty blocks but we still had to wait an hour until he finished work. We drove past the neighbours' place, and into our driveway, and we noticed our beautiful outhouse in distress! We had not even noticed that our neighbours' garage had been flattened by fire. It seems Rollie's kids had not only burned down their old man's garage, they had also levelled our beautiful outhouse. Dad's building days were over. He moved a ramshackle, horrible, outhouse on-site and it was still there when I joined the air force.

Rollie was not my dad's favorite neighbour even though we used his outside water-pump for years. Pa didn't like him for several reasons: Rollie was a Catholic; he had been in the air force, not the army like my Pa; and he cheered for the Maple Leafs, and constantly watched National Hockey League. These were all perfectly good reasons to dislike someone in my dad's view. We kids used to sing "Rollie-Pollie – finger up my holey." I'm not proud of that, but it's the truth. Dad must have heard us, but he ignored our song.

One time, Dad found a half-tame Magpie. I adopted him, and he hung around me forever. The Magpie was on Rollie's clothesline, and Rollie was going to shoot him. The unbelievable happened. Dad pushed past Rollie's wife, and confronted Rollie, who was armed with a shotgun! My old man was mean as a bear, and didn't know the meaning of fear. Mr. Magpie survived!

Somehow, we received a final tax notice. They were going to sell our shack for overdue taxes. Dad was scrounging for money to pay the taxes and Gayle and I, wanted to help out, so we chipped in the money we had earned from distributing fliers for the grocery stores. We each had a coffee before we donated our pay. I don't know why, but we sure felt guilty about having that coffee.

Dad knew who was trying to buy our house. It was a fool walking down the road. Dad uttered, "That S.O.B.," and was going to run over him. He only stopped after he saw us crying, and heard Ma screeching. The bargain hunter lived.

I delivered groceries using my old bike with the steel carrier. I also joined an Army Cadet Corps, at my old man's suggestion.

"You should join the army," he said. "They would smarten you up."

I guess the cadet corps didn't cut it. For some reason, never explained, Pa gave me an ultimatum; I had to choose the Cadet Corps, or the grocery delivery job. It was one, or the other. I had just joined cadets, and I had to quit. I needed the money from my grocery delivery route. Go figure!

Dad's railway pass whisked me to New Westminster, but the trip was not without incident. To get there, I had to change trains in MacLeod before heading west to New Westminster. Even though I had Ma's wrist watch pinned to me, I slept through my stop. The conductor said that I had told him that I was going to Lethbridge. He had obviously not seen me sleeping in my seat. It was CYA (cover your ass) time for him! He dropped me off in the middle of the night, at a nearly-deserted station, in Lethbridge. A Travelers' Aid lady offered me a room for the night. She said she would only charge one dollar, if I could afford it. I willingly spent some of my limited funds in a hurry. The next morning this wonderful lady walked me to the station. There really are some good people in this world!

I finally ended up in New Westminster, the next night, again, in the middle of the night. I got off the train and looked for the Bus Depot. I could only find a place called "Pacific Stage Lines". I was young, and scared. I had seen enough cowboy movies to know what a stage coach was. Traditional historic names are great but it would have been nice if they had explained to this twelve-year-old that the place they called Stage Company was actually the bus station. In the meantime, I wasn't gettin' on 'no stage coach!'

A cop thought I was a young runaway. I showed him my train pass. He confirmed that the Stage Company was actually a bus company. I still wasn't convinced so I confirmed it with the ticket agent.

The bus flew over the Pattullo Bridge, toward White Rock. My stop was at Scott Road. There was nothing there. The driver waited as long as he could. He tried to get me to stay on the bus until I could get some help. Nope! I got off the bus. His taillights disappeared. I felt abandoned. Then I heard, "Ken-nee, Ken-nee, Ken-nee". My big Aunt Frances came through after all. Good old Aunt Frant! WHAT A TRIP! I hit the bed, and passed out, exhausted, ready to start my summer holidays.

Back home, in the fall, we had unseasonably wet weather and the dugout, under the house, flooded. My job was to take a hand-pump and pump the water out. It took over one hour of steady pumping until I heard it sucking on the bottom. Pa was trying to clear the muck, and he snapped. He grabbed me by the legs, and I thought he was, literally, going to drown me. My foot caught him on the side of the head and he let go. I got out of there. It was the only time I ever had to defend myself against him. We never spoke about it, and this is the first time I've ever told anyone that story.

Chapter Six

First Jobs - Growing Up Fast - Discovery
of 'Negroid Extraction'

As little kids, Gayle and I were largely unsupervised, and we liked to go exploring. One rainy fall weekend, we got down an ornate, metal, chocolate box from the shelf. It had a pair of beautiful Mallard ducks painted on its lid.

Our 'Duck Box' was full of old pictures and not-so-important papers. We had snooped through that box many times. This time, we came across a document that Grandpa had kept. It was his gun licence. The paper listed his name, address, age and racial Origin. The paper said he was of 'Negroid Extraction'.

What the hell was this? We were bowled over! We thought we were white! That damned Duck Box! If it weren't for that box, and our discovery, that day, I would have gone on in life thinking I was white!

The reality set in that day. It explained why we were hanging around scuzzy east Calgary. It also explained why we had some many visitors, in the form of well-dressed black men.

It was very confusing to us. My little sister once stroked a visiting black gentleman's hand and said "dirdee" (dirty). My racist father put a stop to all those visits in a hurry.

Kids are colour blind when it comes to their parents. Ma wasn't as slim, or as well cared for, as she had been in her younger years. Her Negroid characteristics jumped out at us. Our imagination didn't help. We weren't white; we weren't black. We were Zebras!! All the remarks we heard about Negroes flooded back. We had made some of those remarks ourselves. We were nauseated. We had laughed as racial insults were hurled at others. It wasn't so funny now.

You can't know, unless you've been there, how scathing the word nigger is, and how deeply it cuts. You cry in frustration.

"It's not my fault," you keep saying. Then you ask yourself, "Why in the hell is the word 'fault' even being used? It's a biological fact."

Tears soon turn to anger and rebellion, then just anger at everything, and everybody! We were in limbo. We were afraid to discuss 'it,' or anything else, with our parents. We just simmered.

Meanwhile, Ma suggested that I get a job so I could pay board. It sounded okay with me. But I never would have thought of quitting school; I was a bright student. Ma objected, insisting that if I could get a job, with a future, I should quit school. She then left the want ad page folded open in the paper. I was fifteen years, eleven months and twenty-eight days old, when I saw the ad. She must have seen the ad, and set me up.

The Bank of Montreal was looking for an Entrant-In-Training. They wanted someone who was academically-inclined, sixteen-years-old or older, with a minimum Grade Ten requirement. I put on my best, and only, good suit, the one I wore to Grade Nine graduation, and went for an interview.

They must have thought they had another John D. Rockefeller, in the rough, on their hands, so I was hired right away. After I had completed all the testing, I started work on September 4, 1955 which was also my sixteenth birthday. It was a great program. In those days, the bank promoted mostly within the company, and they would provide an employee with free high school courses, and training.

I could get on the bus for student fare. A lot of people must have thought I was a geek. Who else would wear a blue suit to school?

People who were refined, and well-mannered, people were new to me. Rules and guidelines, I would find out later, were also a problem for me.

Because we were going to be future executives, we were treated to a dinner in the Palliser Hotel in Calgary; it was one of the most regal hotels in the area. One kid was so nervous that, when he selected a dinner roll, one got loose and bounced down the table, and landed in our host's soup. I've never since anyone who had such a red face. We kind of snickered.

Our branch had nine people in it. All of the men, including me, had keys. One of the other young tellers, and I, used to take a pellet pistol, and shoot up cardboard targets for practice in the basement. Apparently, the police used to sponsor handgun safety, and range practice, for bank employees. This practice stopped before I was on staff. We were told that, in case of a robbery, we were to hand over the money and not be heroes.

One day, the accountant and I, took $10,000 to Main Office. The accountant left me, and the ten grand, in the car with a revolver so he could buy some shoes. Tempted or what? I was getting paid thirty dollars a week. My board and room cost forty-five dollars per month at home.

I hung around with a real tough kid named Walter. Walter, me, and another one of my friends, liked to go into a riding academy's field, and ride their small Shetland ponies at night. Lanky Walter got astride one small pony. We swore his feet almost dragged on the ground. We never had halters, bridles, or saddles. On one of these excursions, the horse turned sharply, and Walter flew off, hitting his tailbone on a stump. He writhed in pain; it looked good on him. My other buddy, and I, had a good laugh but Walter didn't think it was so funny.

Walter, and I, once launched a huge cable spool, which was larger than a wagon wheel, sending it over a cliff. We got it going down the hill, lickity-split; it ended up half-way across the shallow Elbow River.

My folks encouraged me to buy a television set on the 'never – never' plan. They didn't have TV and they had revolving credit at Nagler's Department Store. I got the smallest television they had. I thought I could pacify, or please my old man, by buying him stuff. I even bought myself a 12-gauge shotgun, and Pa used it. He still was mean and miserable.

In Dogpatch, the right-of-passage, at age sixteen, was to have a driver's licence; if you didn't have a licence, you were considered lame. I bought a 1939 Chevy Coupe for fifty dollars -- no insurance required.

I parked the Coupe down the street, and I secretly learned how to drive. The problem was that I had the neighbourhood kid, Mikey, in tow and somebody called the fuzz.

"Go home Mikey, "I shouted, and he streaked for his house.

"Where are your license plates?" the cop asked.

I told him I didn't have any.

"Where is your licence?"

I told him I didn't have one. Then, the cop wanted to know where my father was. At this point, I was wishing I didn't have one of them, either!

The cop said he wanted to use our phone to phone Pa, who was visiting at my uncle's house.

"The phone wires were installed but the phone isn't hooked up," I told him. I guess I was so scared he believed me.

"Pa's going to kill me," I kept repeating.

The cop thought I was being dramatic; he didn't know it was a real possibility. A young army neighbour told the cop that he had taken the car out a few times himself, to ensure it was safe. That must have been what the busybody had seen. The army neighbour lied, saying that this was the first time that I had driven it. That army private saved my 'privates' that day! That was close.

The other problem was that my folks knew the man who had previously owned the car. They knew him; I didn't. Ma kept looking across the street, and half-way down the block.

"Isn't that George's car?" she asked.

I honestly could say I didn't know a George. She repeatedly hit Pa with the same question. Finally, they figured it out.

"It's your car, right?"

I proudly admitted ownership, and had the stuffing knocked out of me. Every day, Pa would demand that I sell the car. Every day, I would face up to his brutality. Finally, I decided to keep the car, and move out of the house. One of the few non-violent families in the neighbourhood took me in. Actually there were two families who didn't abuse their kids. What a track record for Dogpatch.

Even though I kept up the payments for the television, it was still at the folks' house. I got fed up, strolled across their living room floor, and unplugged the TV, leaving Pa staring at a blank screen. I started lugging it across the floor.

"Put it back! Plug it in!" said Pa, sounding like a bull moose. "You will wait until my show is over."

I waited a couple of minutes until the show was finished.

"Now get the hell out of here and take your g-d TV with you!"

I exited without my dignity, but at least I had my TV. I only saw Pa periodically after that. One day, surprise of surprises, the old man offered to teach me how to drive. This was his one big peace offering to me. I got behind the wheel and he started with the lesson. I tuned him out, put the clutch in, then put it in first gear, and let the clutch out. I tramped it.

I already knew how to drive. I guess he thought I had an attitude, and he flew into another rage.

I got the plates on the Chevy, and practised for my driver's test. The first challenge was to park between four stakes; I guess this test was designed to save dented fenders. Success! Then I had to take the car test, which was held in downtown traffic.

Eureka! One more to go. Then came parallel parking. I aced it.

Twenty minutes later, I had my licence -- and left a black paint stain down a guy's fender. He was really calm. His wife didn't quite respond the same way. She was a strident crow!

I followed him to a body shop where the repairman fixed the minor damage. It was a good lesson for me. I needed that. It sure smartened me up. Maybe, I decided, it was time to grow up after all.

I had an attitude when it came to the bank courses. I would write the exams, and had great results, but I wouldn't do any of their asinine lessons. It came to a head when the managers decided to enforce the rules about doing all the lessons. I was told to do the assignments, or I couldn't write the exam.

About now, you have probably guessed that my banking career wasn't headed for the stars. You would be right.

I was small in stature and very unsure of myself. I did learn about a technique we called 'kiting'. This doesn't fit today's high rolling defini- tion. When we were broke, we would go to the Chinese grocery store down the street where we could write a personal cheque. The owner's account was in another bank. It would take a good week to clear. By the time it came in – voila! Our pay was in. We were warned about using this practice, but the bank never enforced the rule.

I got to know one of our dry goods retailers and supplemented my income by making deliveries across Calgary for him. I loved driving. This hobby paid for my gas and I could pocket a few bucks for myself.

What's that old joke?

"You can't fire me because I quit!"

It didn't get that far, but my lack of interest in handling other people's money made my departure from the bank inevitable.

I got an enlistment application for the navy. Being a 'prairie chicken' made the thought of exotic places, and lots of water, appealing to me. Pa wasn't so enthusiastic. Imagine my surprise, when I visited my Pa for his signature (I was underage) and he ripped up the application, and physically pushed me out the door. I had the navy blues for about a week. I knew I couldn't show up at the recruiting office for another form. The excuse that the 'dog ate it!' might have worked in school, but it wouldn't cut it in the military.

So I tried the air force. My folks' signatures miraculously appeared on the form. My estranged relationship with my parents was my secret around the bank. I told two motherly-type tellers at the bank about my ambitious plans, and future adventures, so they witnessed my parents' signatures (after I explained that I had forgotten to get witnesses).

I had a preliminary interview which made me late coming back from lunch at the bank. This was the first time I was late in a year-and-a-half. "Where were you Mr. McKnight?" my boss asked, sarcastically. (I was seventeen and he called me 'Mister'.) He got his upper-class nose out of joint when he heard my loud response.

"I was down getting a one way ticket to Montreal, do you mind?"

My basic training was twenty miles from Montreal. Believe me, parting was no great sorrow.

Chapter Seven

First Five Year Hitch in the Military

I was excited to start out on my military adventure. My checkerboard school record caught up with me on my final visit to the recruiting offices.

"Who do you think you are?" the recruiting sergeant asked me. "We take tough guys like you, and make men of them."

Because I went to a different school every year, starting at Grade Four, he thought that I had been kicked out because of discipline problems. He figured I was in dire need of some discipline. I think if I was 'Jack the Ripper' he would have inducted me, anyway.

After surviving my father's wrath, basic training was a walk in the park. I knew the drill NCOs were unlikely to physically assault their recruits. It was like getting a 'get out jail free card'. They yelled and screamed a lot – big deal.

One old warrant officer would stand on a raised platform, and verbally abuse us. I snickered. He was a long way from me, but he paid me a face-to-face visit. He swore, and snarled. I thought to myself, my old man could make you cry, Mr. Warrant Officer.

Dumb insolence was a charge that didn't worry me; I just managed to avoid it.

Rifle drill was next. I found out two things. Don't call it a gun, and don't drop it. The first day I did both. I dropped my gun. I had the rifle gun (I compromised) over my head, and had to run double-time around a large hangar. He made me do this until I should have been exhausted. Lucky for me, he took my smirk as a grimace of pain. I got away with another one.

We all ran around in circles, with our gas masks on, in the gas house, until we were breathing hard. The old sergeant had built up a resistance to tear gas. He took his mask off.

"Masks off everyone. There's no gas in here!" He suckered us. Our eyes welled with tears. Boy, did it sting. A half hour later, we were as good as new.

On graduation day, one recruit dropped his rifle. I couldn't wait. The damn NCO picked it up for him, and gently told him not to be nervous. This Zebra found out in a hurry that the armed forces did not always make sense.

Our boots always had to be immaculate. We discovered that the secret to shiny boots was to brush them with a nylon stocking. My first chance at getting a stocking happened when I was Duty airman. I luckily pulled a sweetheart duty. I had to stand in the back at the movie theatre. If there were any disturbances, my job was to call the 'Meatheads' (Air Force police). My counterpart was the Duty airwoman, and I hit it off. She willingly gave me a nylon stocking. Every night, I treasured it as a trophy when we were all sitting around doing our boots. I felt like a 'lover boy'.

We didn't get much leave in boot-camp. We had parades, and were given enough needles to guard us against every disease known to mankind. We had a Registered Nurse with the rank of Flight Lieutenant who supervised a poor, old, under-trained Leading Aircraftman (bottom of the rank structure) who had to give the needles.

The obvious cure for sore, stiff arms was rifle drill. It worked. My arm muscles already black and blue became numb. Just brilliant!

We had target practice, using .303 rifles, which had its moments. The rifle coach tried to get me, a lefty, to shoot right-handed. Unfortunately, the bolt was on the wrong side for lefties, and the cartridges ejected just past the left-handed person's the face. I waved my weapon around frantically, as I was trying to shoot right-handed. We had live rounds so waving the weapon around saved me trying to reason with the idiot. I shot left-handed, and I still do.

In hindsight, I realize you didn't salute officers when they were driving, except in boot-camp. They said it was good practice. If you didn't, some fool officer would stop his car, chew you out, and report you to the Station Warrant Officer. We wised up in a hurry. If he had a flat hat on, you saluted him. I'd like to have a dollar for every bus driver I saluted. They must have chuckled.

Graduation rolled around. Trade selection was neat. It was supposed to be based on interest, aptitude, and the ability to study. Not so, my friend. They needed thirty Electrical Technicians for Aircraft. All thirty of us fit the bill. Funny, how that worked out.

Then, it was off to Borden. Our 'wet' canteen, on the base, was on federal property – exempt from provincial jurisdiction. There was no age limit until *we* got there. One underage airman got drunk, and ran amok. He threatened the CO's dog, and pounded on the Group Captain's Door. You guessed it: mass punishment! They closed our 'cheap beer' bar to anyone under nineteen.

But we found a loophole. The Orderly Corporal, who was checking IDs, was more interested in selling his fishing flies than really supervising. A couple of nineteen-year-olds would feign an interest in buying them.

The entrance hall, and beer tables, was separated only by coat racks where we hung our trench coats. A few of us used his confusion of selling fishing flies while scanning IDs, to sneak in the beer hall. Once you got in, you were home free.

We had some pick-up hockey teams. That was when I learned hockey socks had no feet in them, just a stirrup. I didn't know an elbow pad from a groin cup. It was an embarrassing night. I was totally out of my element. I never went back to the arena.

One night I slept in my uniform, outside, in the frost. When I got up, you could see the perfect outline of my airman's uniform in frost, everywhere, except for where I had flamed out.

I headed for sick parade; I was hurting. It was the only time, in twenty years, that I 'swung the lead', 'gold-bricked' or faked being sick. My unkempt appearance, and scruffy and crumpled uniform, would have gotten me CB'd (confined to the barracks) for a week which would have meant missing Graduation Day. Before that, for me, my only Graduation had been from Grade Nine.

I wanted to go to British Colombia, but they posted me to Nova Scotia instead. The air force was expanding Greenwood Air Force

Base to accept the Argus, which was a new anti-submarine aircraft. It required a large aircrew, and a horde of ground technicians, to keep it flying. We had a large pool of aspiring technicians who had little to do as our new aircraft had yet to arrive. So we built a golf course! We also performed every manual task that they could think of.

I don't think we had liquor, but the beer flowed freely. We were in a 'dry' county and the liquor laws were archaic.

Oh yes, we had dress parades! You should have seen all the medals on many of the staff. You could hear the inspecting party approaching, as the jingling medals got louder. When the jingling stopped, you knew your superior was about to be eye-ball to eye-ball with you. During these parades, we couldn't wait to hear the fading of the jingling, as they moved further down the rank.

"The further the better," we thought.

We were living in the sticks big time, in rural Nova Scotia. So my buddy, and I, decided to split the cost of a car. Hey, it was better than no car! All we could afford was a 1953 Pontiac even between the two of us. Joe was a real smooth operator, who played the guitar; he was pretty savvy. He truly had the gift of gab. He was dark, and a Zebra, like me. We never mentioned his Negroid features, and he didn't bring it up.

We were the best of roommates. We would rent a local hall, play music and charge a pittance for admission. The local punks were rough, and tough, and they sure didn't like airmen. They resented the fact that most airmen had good clothes, steady paycheques, and a nice club on the base where we could to take our dates. The good ole boys, those local rednecks, would not pay, and they didn't dance, either. Instead, they would try to hassle us. We liked to joke that they spit on the wood stove, and used the F word a lot, but we had no trouble taking their young women to our Airman's Club.

One night, I was working on a crew until midnight with Harvey, a Newfoundlander. I went to an Airman's Club dance after my shift, and hooked up with him. About two o'clock in the morning, we decided to go to Halifax. We could have sworn the road curved around every apple tree. Our trip to Halifax took us two and a half hour hours, along bad roads.

Unbeknownst to me, Harvey was drunk. He had gotten off early, and primed himself with Newfy Screech.

"Jesus Christ Harv, we are going to hit a pole!" I screamed at him. Just then, his old Studebaker turned ninety degrees, and cut the pole off at the bottom. My head went through the windshield, which was a two piece job, with a metal divider, separating each piece. The car started to burn. The doors were jammed. I kicked mine open, and got Harvey out of the driver's side. We crawled up onto the highway. I looked around for Harvey, and he was back in the wreck. He was working feverishly to strip the under-dash wiring out so the fire stopped.

We were taken by ambulance to the Base Hospital. We woke up in hospital beds, side by side. I had a severe headache and a huge black-and-blue bump on my head. My head felt so big! I had hit the metal strip divider head on, and shattered the windshield.

The next morning, we were served scrambled eggs. I soon lost my appetite when Harv's dressing turned into a river of red. The nurses re-stitched him.

They didn't tell me what happened, and I didn't ask. All I knew, was there went my appetite for breakfast, and I didn't eat anything until supper.

The cops came in asking the nurse/matron if we had been drinking. She said the symptoms of shock, and drunkenness, sometimes were very similar. (You wouldn't get away with drinking and driving now, and there is no way you should.)

They released me the next morning; Harv was in for a few more days. I went to survey the damage, and get the wreck towed away. For some reason, a couple young women were there looking at the wreck. I recognized the shy girl, Margaret, because I had met her when I had dated her girlfriend, Gerry. The other one, I don't remember. (Gerry ended up marrying a friend of mine.)

The girls were staying at a cabin on the hospital grounds, where they worked. If they stayed out too late some of their roommates would pin the girls' underwear to the screen door, so that when their late dates dropped them off, the guys would have a good chuckle.

I knew Margaret still worked at the hospital, and I made a date with her. I had one more trip to Halifax, before my date with Margaret took place.

This date was with a dark-haired beauty who was enrolled in nursing school in Halifax. I knew we weren't serious but was surprised when she said, "You should have phoned, Ken. I'm sorry. I can't have you driving all that way for nothing."

She set me up with her girlfriend. This new relationship was going forward, and was going to work out just fine.

Then I had my date with shy, quiet Margaret. Neither of us had a real childhood. She had been a Children's Aid Ward. On her sixteenth birthday, she started working in the Middleton Hospital kitchen. (You may remember I also started working on my sixteenth birthday.)

We were both old beyond our years. We really connected, and that was the end of playing the field, for me. We got serious, in a hurry, and decided to get married.

To get more money, I convinced Joe to buy out my share of the car. This was good – I had more money – but it also meant that I was on 'shanks mare' which means walking. The base was about eight miles from the hospital. I hitchhiked both ways.

Luckily, I knew a Registered Nurse at the hospital. If her shift coincided with mine, she would give me a ride to the base at midnight. She had a big new black Buick. When you hit the curve at the railway track, you were flying. Her driving scared the daylights out of me but it beat walking.

I decided to hitchhike from Nova Scotia, stay two nights in Calgary, and hitchhike back. I'm sure if you attempted this today, you would be robbed, or murdered. I hitched a ride to the Digby ferry with a young woman. Her boyfriend had been in the air force but was now in the Klink. She didn't elaborate and I didn't press for information.

Wearing the uniform helped with rides. I was waiting to board the ferry, when a young crewman approached me. He asked me to bring him a dozen beer. I had time to kill so I took the money and purchased the beer, and put it in my flight bag. Once safely on board, he escorted me to the crew area. We drank beer and he fed me a good meal.

It was a great start to my trip, but it wasn't all a bed of roses. I slept in a ditch one night, and sat my derriere on the floor of a telephone booth, on another night, in the rain. I wanted to get showered, shaved and rested up, so I headed for a motel room in the middle of the night. I wasn't sure if the motel was open, so I tried the door. It was unlocked, and I walked in. No one was there. What a dilemma. I didn't want to leave because, if someone saw me, they could accuse me of burglary, or robbery. I stayed put. The owner was sure surprised the next morning. I told him if he wanted to call the cops, I would wait for them. He realized I was telling the truth, and wished me well. Sure was nice to have a free night! I'm sure that I got a much better reception than his negligent employee got for leaving the door unlocked.

Some drivers would pick me up, go four miles, and turn into a farm lane. I finally learned to ask, "How far are you going?"

I was stuck in Northern Ontario like that.

It was almost two in the morning – no frost, but it was cold. Hurray, a car stopped. Boo! It was a cop! He asked me what I was doing. I thought that it must be obvious so I told him I was waiting for a Greyhound Bus. He, very pointedly, said there wasn't one on that route until eleven o'clock in the morning. "That's why I'm waiting," I said.

He ignored my snide remark, and pointed out the dangers of hitch-hiking. Good thing I was wearing my uniform. The cop finally told me to get in his car to get warm. I wasn't sure whether it was a gesture of goodwill, or a bust. The heat felt good. He drove me to the end of his jurisdiction, and radioed another car. I changed cop cars and was driven toward my destination, this time with no lecture.

I sent Margaret postcards at the end of each day's journey. She still has them. They are over fifty-five years old, and have been well worn, over the years.

The return adventure was much the same and I was sure glad to see my girl again!

This seems the appropriate place to explain why I was hitchhiking to Calgary on such an adventure. When I left home for the military, my sister was the only one with my address, or knowledge of my where-abouts. If you recall, I was only seventeen, and couldn't join the military, without parental consent. My parents had refused to sign, so I had found my own way. My sister had promised she'd never tell where I was. I had told her I would never come home without a written invitation, and an apology. I received the letter, but no apology. That was good enough for me. As I matured, I realized my parents weren't neglectful and abusive. Their behavior was just a sign of ignorance. Besides, I wasn't as tough as I thought I was, either, and I wanted to make amends with my past before entering married life. I wanted my future wife to know them.

I started back home to Calgary to reconnect with my family. I knew that if I got my leave pass stamped in Calgary, at a post office, or police station, that I would be entitled to my leave travel allowance. It was the only cash I could find to finance my wedding. This explains why I was hitchhiking in the first place instead of travelling in luxury – like a bus or something- -- so that I could reunite with the family AND collect finances for the wedding.

*Love Letters on the Trail. Remember when love
could travel on a four cent stamp?*

Ken rolling a cigarette – NOT a 'joint' just to be clear! Last days of bachelorhood!

Impressed? Angry Zebra on Honour Guard practice.

Chapter Eight

Married Life on a 'Shoe-String'

I managed to get my hands on a 1946 beater Chevy. It was a sickening, greenish colour. It got us around, except in Kentville. Many a time, I had the hood up, until it decided to co-operate.

Before I had wheels, Marg and I walked, and talked a lot. We went down to the railway tracks, and over the bridge. We checked out the baseball dugouts at the ball park. It was so hard to be alone when you had no wheels, and very little money. We were frugal until we retired. Not anymore!

I reluctantly told Margaret about my black heritage. She didn't bat an eye. I think she thought that is why I kept my distance from my relatives. I had previously 'fessed up to one young lady about my bi-racial background, and she had said it didn't make any difference to her. However, she never dated me again. Sometimes, honesty sucks.

I had quit running with Joe, but still wanted him to be my best man. What I didn't know was that the local morons had jumped him, and beat his head against a car bumper. He was going to be my best man with two black eyes. He looked like a raccoon. The female medical technicians took Joe over to the MIR (Medical Inspection Room). They put make-up on him which was called mortician's putty. They told him to re-apply it before the wedding. He looked good in the few pictures we could afford to take.

Joe, and I, stayed at a motel the night before the wedding. We had a bachelor party, for two people, and went to bed. We slept in! We panicked, and went to pick up the flowers.

"When do you want them?" the shopkeeper asked.

"Are you kidding? NOW, you fool!" I blurted out.

"You have to order them," She replied.

I got very contrite, in a hurry, and sweet-talked her. She said that she had never heard anything so funny in her life. I wasn't laughing. She got as busy as the Mad Hatter, quickly borrowing bows, and flowers, from other arrangements that had to be delivered later that day. She said our arrangements would be ready in an hour.

I was in damage control.

We floored the Pontiac, and rushed to pick up the women.

In the meantime Margy had phoned the motel. The pea-brained clerk told her we had checked out hours ago. When we arrived to pick her up, my sweet, quiet bride was screaming like a Banshee.

"Do you want to get married or not?" she asked, seething.

"I don't bloody know," I retorted, like any macho man would.

This was our first, and damned near our last, disagreement.

Joe and I went back for the flowers. We stopped on a fork in the road. I looked left and right. On the left was the safety of the base, my haven, and on the right was the fork that led to wedded bliss.

I deliberated for twenty more minutes before I decided we should tie the knot.

Even though Marg's father was poor as a church mouse, and of questionable integrity, we had invited him to the wedding, anyway. It was a real posh affair. The five in attendance included the bride (Margy), the groom (me), the bridesmaid (Marg's sister), Wild Joe (my best man) and Marg's father.

Marg and I often reminisce, and we both still agree that 'flying off the handle' was no way to start a life together.

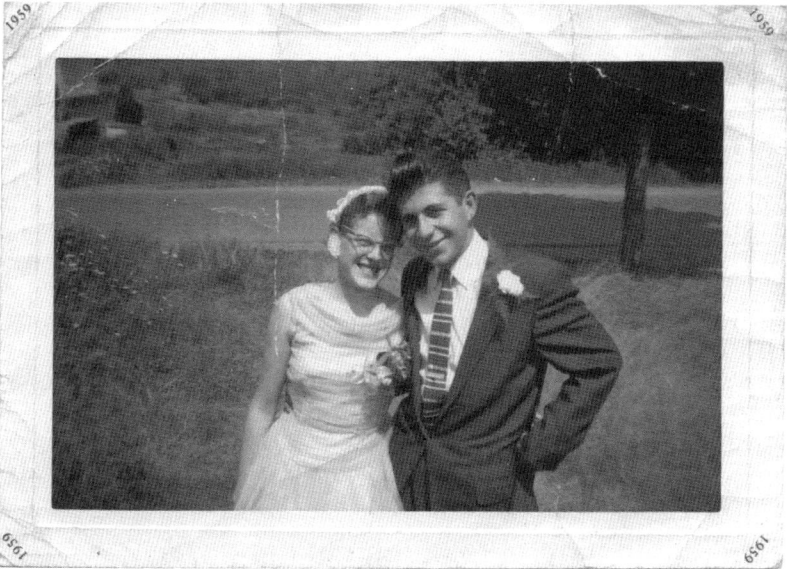

Ken and Marg tie the knot August 15, 1959

A crew mate of mine was moving out of an apartment to a better place. He offered us his small and decrepitly-furnished apartment. We didn't know why he moved out because we were happy there. A buddy set an alarm clock in our bedroom window, and at three in the morning, on our wedding night, it went off. Margaret was not amused.

We were happy until we got flooded out. Apparently, this flooding had happened before, but housing was at a premium. There are some good Nova Scotian landlords, and bad Nova Scotian landlords, but in my experience, the majority stink!

It didn't help that airmen weren't particularly popular. The parents thought we'd take their daughters away, and the local guys thought we'd take away their girls! I loved my job, but I didn't like the totally rural area, and all the hypocritical locals.

We needed another apartment, in a hurry, after we got flooded out. We lucked in. Mr. Chipman rented us the back part of a farmhouse in the sticks. He raised beef, and had an apple orchard. He was great. He used a rototiller to make us a large garden plot. Even though I was a non-farmer, I took advantage of his barn to raise chickens. We had very little money so we were quite content to spend hours in our garden, and tending the chickens.

Marg became pregnant, and I worried that my car wasn't dependable so I arranged for a taxi to provide an express service to the hospital, on short notice. I jokingly told Margaret she could have the baby anytime now, as it was nine months to the day we were married. She had a severe backache so I rubbed her back, but it continually got worse. I called the doctor, and said I thought she was in labour.

"Bring her in NOW," he told me. I was later relieved when the doctor told me that the back problems were part of labour symptoms.

The taxi showed up as promised. The driver had obviously done this before. He had a little Volkswagen bug with the passenger seat removed. He didn't need the front seat as he was often called upon to deliver babies, and called his taxi the 'delivery' bug. We got to the hospital and Marg delivered our son. He was a beautiful child. We named him John David McKnight. Another young airman's wife gave birth at the same time. Skip, and I, kept in touch after he took his release. He ended up at GM in Oshawa.

I was fortunate to be able to drive Marg, and our little son, home. I was happy that I could spend a few days with my family before departing for Greenland.

My job was to service the four-engine Argus anti-submarine aircraft. When on operations, it was loaded with torpedoes, depth charges, and bombs. It was an adventure to go on a test flight with one. We'd fly fifty feet above the ocean, from each direction, to check out the anti-submarine detectors' apparatus.

Our crew had a meeting to discuss an operation at Thule, Greenland. In the summertime, the sun never sets up there, and the landscape is all gravel and rock, void of any vegetation. The place also gets fogged in for days at a time.

They wanted volunteers; My hand was the only hand that shot up. I now know why they say to never volunteer for anything in the air force! As a rule, if they send rookies like me, we are accompanied by an experienced technician. No such luck. I was the only aircraft electrical technician on the trip.

Needless to say, I was pretty nervous. The Argus was a huge aircraft with all new technology. It was the first alternating current aircraft in our fleet. In preparation for this exciting expedition, I went through all the records, all the files on past problems, and recorded them all in my notebook. I was ready!

I sat in the bombardier's plastic 'blister'. Spectacular! You had to crawl on your hands, and knees, through a 'tunnel' to access it. It was eerily quiet. The engines were far behind me. It would have been a rush to stay in the blister on landing, but if anything happened to the under-carriage, you would have been squashed like a bug. Safety regulations prohibited occupancy during take offs and landings.

We landed with very few technical glitches. We found one during the between-flight inspection, a cargo door warning light came on. Fortunately, I had the troubleshooting procedures down pat. It was an easy fix. Wow, was I relieved; it would have grounded the aircraft. I didn't need another technician flown in to help me; that would have been totally embarrassing.

I couldn't wait to get home to play with my new son. My wife, and I, spent some time with him, and put him in his crib. The next day, we found him dead. I tried to give him mouth to mouth. I really wasn't sure how, but I tried everything. It was to no avail. He was truly gone. We were devastated.

The next few days were an unreal blur for both of us. We were full of questions, and guilt. The autopsy found the cause of death was instant pneumonia. I was half out of my mind with grief.

"Don't tell me, you son of a bitch," I screamed at the medical exam-iner when he called to give me the results.. "Tell my wife!"

He was a lot nicer than I was. He got Marg on the phone, and explained there was nothing we could have done to prevent it. We were relieved because we felt were green about kids. Still, it was small conso-lation. Looking back, we got some comfort from his words, but at that time, we were so racked with guilt, and grief, he couldn't reason with us. That was fifty-four years ago, but visiting his grave in Middleton, Nova Scotia today still takes a toll on us. Zebras, whites, blacks - we all grieve.

John David – son – 1960 – Such grief to bear.

We survived; somehow, we always do. We sure worked the garden that season. I had seen so much grief that year; I couldn't even kill my chickens and asked my neighbor to help me. I could do it today, if I had to, but I got out of the chicken business in a hurry.

We thought a new apartment would save us the dreaded walk into our son's room. It helped a bit – so did time.

I took my trade exams seriously this time. I took a lot of things more seriously. The pay improved so much you could live on it. I bought a new 1960 model 850 Austin Mini for $1,325 on the never-never plan meaning the payments were so small I'd never get it paid off.

We knew we couldn't replace our son, but we realized we wanted another baby. So Marg became pregnant, again.

We corresponded with my folks, in Dogpatch, and arranged a visit. It wasn't an easy trip for a pregnant woman -- 2,200 miles, one way, in an 850 Austin Mini – it wasn't exactly luxury travel! I paid for the trip by laying sod, washing beer glasses, and picking apples. I worked for Marg's uncle laying sod. I was family, and got one dollar an hour. I don't know what casual help got; I hate to think what that might have been!

Our trip to Alberta was excellent. For the first time in my life, I got along with my parents. They thought Marg was too good for me. Maybe they were right. In any case, she fit in better than I did. On the way back, we stopped in front of a bar in Manitoba. The locals were mesmerized by my little Austin 850. They invited us in for a friendly beer. We graciously declined. I had visions of those strapping farmers placing my car on the flat roof of the bar to 'test' the weight of my Mini.

The mini performed perfectly all the way out, and back. I drove nearly all that distance accident-free until I slowed for a one-way bridge, near home, and some babe rear-ended me. Go figure. Not much damage except to her pride. We were one mile away from home.

By the time we arrived home, we were beginning to recover from the loss of our son. The void was partially filled with the arrival of my cute little daughter. Carol Ann was born January 15, 1962. We couldn't have been happier. To help pay some expenses, Marg agreed to work for an older lady in a wheelchair. She offered us reduced rent if Marg would look after her. I thought that I could shoulder most of the burden of lifting, and caring for her, but she expected Marg to do everything for her, and didn't want my help. That would have been too much for a young mother, so we had to move again.

Luckily, we finally got settled in military permanent married quarters (P.M.Q.s). Wow, here we were, in a new townhouse, with reasonable rent. For two underprivileged young married people, the world was ours.

We let nature take its course, and to our delight, we had another son. It's hard to put this in print, but here goes: Our second son also died as an infant. Nowadays they call it Sudden Infant Death Syndrome, or S.I.D.S

Kenneth John – second son – 1963. It's too much sadness.

We did a lot of soul-searching. The question still haunts us. Why? I told the coroner I didn't want this son all cut apart by an autopsy, like the other son. He said it was the law. I screamed that he must think I murdered my son; I was inconsolable.

The graves are almost side-by-side. We tell ourselves that the fellow, whose marker is between them, keeps an eye on both of them. Even all these years later, we are still trying to put these tragedies behind us. Writing this segment of my autobiography is gut-wrenching; it's as vivid as it was fifty years ago but it is helping me come to grips with that terrible period of my life.

These kinds of tragedies make all the racial intolerance I've been subjected to more tolerable. Racial intolerance is still senseless, and preventable with education. Our tragedies with our beautiful babies were not!

Chapter Nine

Argus Anti-Submarine Aircraft Adventures

I spent seven years working on the Argus – that state-of-the-art anti-submarine aircraft in Greenwood, Nova Scotia. Those years took me on a few exotic adventures. We worked closely with the American Navy whose crewmen looked after the submarine hunting and sub-chasing in the States.

We dealt with the aviation wing of their navy. Our roles were exactly the same. We both chased submarines. They were still flying the P2-V7 Neptunes. My first test flight was on a Neptune.

One incentive for us was 'Risk Pay' which provided thirty dollars per month when your turn came around, less income tax, of course. I guess the way the aircrews figured, if you were willing to fly in the aircraft, then the maintenance must have been excellent.

We each had to sign out a life preserver, called a Mae West, and a para-chute harness. The Safety Equipment Technicians had to size the harness which went between your legs. They delighted in jerking it, oh so tight. A couple of times, I was worried about a sex change.

On one trip, we sat on the floor of the Neptune, with our backs against the large gas tank. In a roar, we were airborne, and all hell broke loose. It got our attention; what a racket. Then came an eerie silence except for the throbbing of the engines and we could breathe again.

Hold the phone, it was only one engine! The other one had severe damage, and was shut down. We didn't realize it – thankfully, ignorance was bliss. The pilot landed shortly after take-off. We complained about the short joy ride. That is, until we discovered he had performed a one-engine emergency landing. It was a smooth landing – what a pilot!

We had a great relationship with our American counterparts, who often acted as the host squadron. One time, the Yanks took us to Marineland, Florida – this was before Canada had its own Marineland, in Niagara Falls. They even paid all of our ticket fees.

Our host station was Jacksonville Naval Air Station. One aircrew Petty Officer owned a bar, in Jacksonville, and he wouldn't let us buy even one round. We received the same treatment at Patuxent River, Maryland. They even arranged guided tours through the White House in Washington, D.C.. We also had a sobering trip to Arlington Military Cemetery.

We were involved, up to our necks, in the Cuban Missile Crisis in 1962, so much so, that we were told to say goodbye to our wives and kids.

We were on one hour standby alert. We would then have to deploy all of our aircraft where they wouldn't become a primary target.

"Where are we going?"

"Sorry, it's classified."

"How long will we be gone?"

"Sorry, it's classified."

They made mushroom techs out of us. They fed us horseshit, and kept us in the dark.

Few people realize what a great man John F. Kennedy was. He made a secret pact to remove all missiles from Turkey. And then, the U.S.S.R. agreed to pull their missiles out of Cuba. This prevented Armageddon. However, I vowed to never go to Cuba as long as that Communist Regime continued in power.

Probably, the best men I ever worked for were the corporals from all the aircraft trades in Greenwood, Nova Scotia. We all worked together. You would have been a darn fool not to listen to their suggestions or advice. I had little respect for the ranks beyond the rank of corporal. I wished the corporals every success.

I didn't have wonderful experiences with the Warrant Officers that I met, then, and I still don't. It might have been my 'attitude'! On most operations, away from base, everyone pitched in – except for our fear-less Warrant Officer.

The Warrant Officer on our Puerto Rican detachment was deathly afraid of scorpions. It didn't help matters that one of the ground crew had got stung a week before. In Puerto Rico, the American Navy had a large medical staff, and had all the antidotes. The guy was very sick but was in little danger of dying.

Our 'leader' would get off the bus and high tail it to the crew chief's tent because we were in the jungle. He wore coveralls, and tightly taped the bottoms of the legs. He would then sit in the chair with his feet on the desk. I guess he thought he was scorpion-free.

The last day of our exercise, he decided to help out by pulling a heavy energizer machine, by hand. The energizer powers electricity to the aircraft, and was self-propelled, but he didn't know it. We let him pull his guts out before we showed him how to operate it.

We were told to keep the aircraft flying but we could also enjoy the beaches. My junkets took me to Bermuda, Puerto Rico, and the Canary Islands. Most of these exercises on any given year, took place in the month of February. It's really novel to land on a tropical island, in the Canaries, and see this huge Christmas tree sticking out of the sand on a beach. They have many Scandinavian tourists, and they do this every Christmas.

I recall, vividly, my adventures on the Argus.

One time, we were running up the engines, with four props whizzing around. A small private aircraft taxied behind us and, we looked back to see that little aircraft tipping up on one wing, and then righting itself. Then it went nose first into the tarmac, smashing its prop. It looked like an ostrich with his head in the sand. The pilot was really shook up.

"Didn't you see our navigation lights?" we asked.

"Yes," he said, "But I thought you were shutting down."

He was only flying across the Bay of Fundy to St. John, New Brunswick for a romantic rendezvous with his girl. He didn't get there! Such is life.

We witnessed about one incident a year. One time, I was gawking out the hangar doors when a goose (Argus) came running up, and its left undercarriage collapsed. What a bang. At least one port engine was trashed, and the prop had some awful curves in it.

The Argus holds over 6,000 gallons of fuel. In an emergency, the fuel has to be jettisoned before landing. On a maintenance check, these valves have to be tested, and then operated. One time, one valve stuck open; the fuel was immediately jettisoned. The whole area around the aircraft was saturated with 115/145 octane aircraft gasoline.

A modification followed shortly, when we were able to plug the jettison tubes with wooden plugs which were about the size of a small fence post. These plugs would allow only a trickle of fuel to come out. This allowed the system to be fully checked without the worry of a gasoline flood, and heaven forbid a fuel fire or explosion.

Shortly after the Argus arrived, a friend of mine was on a test flight, and the nose wheel got stuck in the 'up' position and the aircraft also developed a fuel leak. They took a fire axe, and chopped a hole in the floor, and a flight engineer was lowered down on a rope. He kicked the nose gear free, and it locked into the 'wheels down safe position'.

In those days, everyone smoked; with a fuel leak, no one smoked. My friend was a little more nervous on his next test flight.

Another time, Harvey, an aero-engine technician, was 'running up' the Argus engines. I was the only other person on the aircraft because I had some electrical equipment to check out. I looked out the emergency hatch on the port (left) wing and saw that the whole side of the aircraft was in flames. I informed Hard.

He already knew it because of the ground-man's observations. He told me to relax; because he had simply over-primed the engines, and we had to keep them running. The prop wash kept the flames contained until the excess fuel had burned off. I don't know if he was smart, or lucky, but he was right. I told him he could get another electrician for his next pyrotechnic display. I had no intention of becoming a 'crispy critter'!

Tragedies don't limit themselves to aircraft. One day, a snow plough took a pass close to the hangar doors, and hit a crew chief who suffered a ruptured spleen, and other severe injuries. He passed away shortly afterward. It was a sad day at Greenwood.

Chapter Ten

Military Postings

Margaret and I were discussing our next transfer. We knew it was imminent as I had been at Greenwood for six, or seven, years. I sure had mixed feelings about leaving my 'pet' aircraft but I was happy to leave rural Nova Scotia, and what I thought were its backward ways.

I began to ponder ways to improve my chances on 'civvy' street after I finished my military years. A transfer, I thought, might bring some release from our grief at the loss of our sons; perhaps it could be the change that would allow me to pursue further education.

Over the winter, I decided I would start working on my teacher's certificate. I started off with Grade Ten science. Boy, I had a long way to go. I remember one of the first experiments. Basically, a 115 volt lamp cord was severed, and both bare halves were placed in a single container of water. Now water alone is NOT a good electrical conductor. If you add salt, and stir like crazy, the salt water becomes a great conductor. Want to try it? If you're not careful, the lamp would light up, and so would you.. I don't how many people received electrical shocks with this one experiment. I know if I wasn't a qualified electrician, I would have gotten a jolt.

Marg was very supportive, and encouraging, about my long-range career plans. I thought everyone would be. I told an older friend, and he gave me a lecture about how nice it was to dream, but he thought that the real world would place so many obstacles in my way that I couldn't succeed. I don't think he was being mean. He actually believed it. I just got more determined, but I never told anyone else. I decided I would do my twenty years in the air force; I only had another fourteen years to go!

I reckoned that my pension, and rehab leave, would pay for teacher's college. I just had to make sure that all my other education requirements would be met.

When I was transferred, I hoped that I would have a new start, a change of venue and that there would be less visibility, and reminders of our losses. I told Marg I'd go anywhere but 6 R. D. Trenton. Trenton I liked – 6 R.D. (Repair Depot) I didn't like. Guess what? I got transferred to 6 R.D. on the Air Base in Trenton.

On the way to Trenton, we stopped at Marg's grandmother's place in Port Williams, near the Minas Basin. When we arrived, her uncle looked at me, and told me some horrendous news.

"Ken," he said. "You have lost one of your bombers."

I didn't want to believe him, but it was true. An Argus crashed into the ocean off Puerto Rico during an anti-submarine exercise. There were no survivors, and there was very little wreckage including the fridge. It took me a long time to get over that tragedy.

In the air force, we were supposed to have a career manager – we called them 'career manglers'. I never heard of one for the first twelve years of my career. Seems that my career manager thought I'd love the Trenton 6 R.D. According to the old hands, the R.D. was the "Old Man's Retirement Home". The old guys loved it. They said that you stayed there until you retired, or died, right there at 'Dead Man's Plot'. The guys worked straight days with every weekend off. What's not to like?

I'll tell you! It was the stinking job itself.

There was no bloody way I was feeling THAT old! I thought I was still a young buck! After working on anti-submarine bombers, the letdown was immense. I had taken great pride in the Argus. "Keep 'em flying" was our old saying. We lived it and we loved it!

The lowly 6 R.D. job involved working on old scrap-worthy aircraft; it didn't turn my crank. Some of our bosses were civilians, who had the authority of Sergeants and Warrant Officers. However, they didn't march in parades or take on temporary duty or, 'Joe Jobs,' such as 'Duty Warrant Officer', 'Orderly Sergeant', etc. The 'civvies' weren't required to have neat clothes, or haircuts, so they weren't required to 'lead by example'. It was sure hard on morale but I tried to make the best of a bad situation.

My first inkling that there was patronage at 6 R.D. was after I was there for a few weeks. We had been living in a motel. Just after we moved in to the tiny town of Frankford, they sent me on temporary duty to Cold Lake, Alberta.

Marg didn't drive, and didn't know a soul. I know what they say that if you can't take a joke then you shouldn't have joined up. But guess what! My wife didn't join up. She was the one being put through the wringer, needlessly. There were other guys on the duty list whose turn it was to go on temporary duty. I didn't expect to get manipulated by a few bosses with no common sense or humanity. Guess the 'brown-nosers' won that round.

We were re-assembling CF104s in Cold Lake. It was an important task and, probably, someone who had worked on 104s, or fighter air-craft, would have been more qualified. I was a fast learner, and acquired a new skill set that was required very quickly.

A guy in our wet canteen happened to be black. A few guys called him 'Snowball'. I objected, and was told to butt out. I did. I had enough crosses to bear. Those idiots were convinced that the moniker 'Snowball' didn't offend him. Some suggested he even liked it. What a bunch of redneck crap.

The only saving grace about temporarily living in Cold Lake was that I finally established a relationship with my father, in Alberta. He had a bad heart - he had one after all! I visited him a couple of times in Calgary. The padre found me in my barracks. Dad had succumbed to a heart attack. It made me glad that I hadn't gone over my immediate boss's head to duck out of that temporary duty back at the 6 R.D. or I would have missed the opportunity to revisit my relationship with my father.

The padre arranged for me to get a training flight from Cold Lake to Edmonton. He strongly urged the pilot to extend the flight to Calgary for me. The pilot had the final say, and he refused to do it. Most people, even officers, would have done it because of a death in the family.

So I had to hitchhike from Edmonton to Calgary. On my first ride, I related my story about the bum deal to the driver, and he drove me right to the front door of Ma's house. He wouldn't take any money. He, too, had been an enlisted man, who was plagued by the, 'I-don't-give-a-damn officers'. Fortunately, those kinds of people were in the minority, but the bad-asses have too much clout when human decency is required.

My father's funeral was, really, a family reunion. I saw aunts, and uncles, I hadn't seen for years. It was late spring – even in Calgary, it was too late for snow. My big Aunt Frant looked out the window, on the day of the funeral, and sure enough – there was six inches of snow on the ground. My semi-religious aunt let fly with more profanities than I heard in boot-camp! We split our sides laughing. We were all wound pretty tightly and she sure relieved the tension. Even my religious, dour, Aunt Lil had to smile.

After the funeral, my engineering officer, who eventually became a Lt. Colonel, made me produce an obituary notice from the paper that reported my father's death. It was pretty tacky – but typical -- I would say. Who would believe this stuff? They seemed to think, if you were an enlisted man, you were mostly animal. Did I mention that, years later, this inhumane S.O.B. was caught trying to load his sailboat onto a Hercules? I think he was court-martialed. What goes around comes around.

Two of us finished our tour at Cold Lake and, before departure we were visited by a new, young, engineering officer. I think he stuck his neck out for us, because he told us to take our orders and disappear from the base until our air transportation departure time in Edmonton. I headed for Calgary to Ma's for a visit.

The other fellow was celebrating the end of his tour. He was buying the beer for his buddies in the mess. The 'meat heads' (military police) walked in. He had new orders. He was to stay in Cold Lake, and his old orders were rescinded. They didn't catch me until just before my flight time in Edmonton. They had taken my name off the flight manifest, with no explanation. I was told to return to Cold Lake for duty. It was another corporal, just like me, who was manning the desk. This was the last straw. I unloaded on him. Luckily, he put my name back on the flight. If he had called a superior, I would have been back in Cold Lake, or in the slammer.

I breathed a sigh of relief when our transport aircraft retracted its undercarriage. Wheels up, and we were airborne. The next day, I was processing my travel claim receipts in Trenton. A civilian woman - 6 R.D. Style - got pretty snotty with me.

"So you're the one that got away," she said.

I played stupid. She then went on to say that I should be sent right back to Cold Lake. I assured her I didn't know what she was talking about. Who? Me? I told her I always followed orders. If I should get an order cut for me, of course, I would gladly go back to Cold Lake. What a line that was! Even 6 R.D. was better than being in Cold Lake, all alone. She sputtered, and said something that either I wasn't worth it, or that sending me out there for another few days wasn't worth it. Who cared? I was back home with my wife, and daughter.

Three of us villains were plotting how to avoid the life sentence at 6 R.D. The instrument technician, in our trio, saw a bulletin, the Daily Routine Orders (DROS), that said that electrical and instrument technicians were needed for the highly technical Flight Simulator Trade. He applied and was readily accepted. Needless to say, the other two of us, with electrical expertise, followed.

Right. There were no flight simulators at 6 R.D. If I could pass the course, then my life sentence was over. I passed the test after only a year and a half. Life was good again.

Chapter Eleven

New Trade - New Hope - Entrepreneurial Ventures

I announced my decision to my wife. The course was five months long at Camp Borden, close to Barrie, Ontario. The air force thought I would be stuck up there, and commuting on the weekends. I made "mushroom technicians" out of them. Once again, I fed them horseshit and kept them in the dark.

Marg and I didn't want to be separated again. I guess the uncertainty of the Cuban Missile Crisis was still in the back of our minds. The old saying, "Forgiveness is easier to get than permission," has a lot of validity. I boldly stored my junky furniture in a friend's basement, and drove my wife, and daughter, up to Angus, Ontario, just outside of Base Borden. I found a nice furnished apartment by the end of the next day. Some say it was blind luck. I say good planning! Carpe diem. Seize the day.

As an aside: Before the transfer, we were on a broom-ball team. I was a terrible player, so I was stuck in goal. We were losing 11 to 0. The opposition was out for blood. I had a short fuse. Their star player was always scoring on me, while his 'joe-boy' was sticking his broom in my face. I cracked him across the collar bone, with my broom. He dropped to the ice. He finally got up, and verbally threatened me. I don't blame him. My other two villains kept him away from me on the ice. They played defence. I thought he might line me up in the parking lot. Sure glad he didn't as he was 'Mr. Athlete'. My fellow villains and I were very close after that.

I found the course extremely difficult. Most of my classmates were years younger. They had updated electronics training. Fortunately for me, the whiz-bangs helped me out immensely.

We all passed. I was trained. Goodbye Camp Borden. Hello Ottawa. The Canadian Forces Base Uplands was my new home. The air force was installing a state-of-the-art Hercules Flight Simulator at CFB Uplands. The air base, and international airport, shared the runways just outside of Ottawa.

I couldn't find a place to live. I had applied everywhere, but to no avail. So I looked up the same older cousin who did so much for us when we were kids. I had 'helped' her husband, Ted, build their house in Edmonton when I was young. Just being six- or seven-years-old, I'm sure I was more trouble than 'help'. Ted was an articulate, educated gentleman. He had been a senior civil servant in Edmonton, and took a lot of ribbing because he was from the East. They put us up, and finally got us a good apartment, in a high rise, until we moved into a newer semi-detached P.M.Q. It was our dream home. Very few enlisted men could afford to buy a home in the 1960's.

I was reunited with my former Flight Simulator classmates after a month's leave. The blood, sweat and tears of my challenging course were well worth it. Another dream had come true.

Someone started a speaking club on the base. It was held in the airmen's dining room (mess hall). It sounded great. The club was meant to help us develop confidence, and be able to field impromptu questions. The club's primary goal was help us to deliver convincing genuine speeches. I took to it like a duck to water. One important aspect of the club was that it let you leave your rank outside the door; there was no intimidation and no perks because of rank. I felt empowered.

My first, and only speech, was directed at people like me --high school drop-outs! I told the audience that being a drop out didn't have to be their final status in life. It was fine to stay in the air force for twenty years. But it was also important to spend every year upgrading your high school education and working on a degree, or certificate, for Community College. Ottawa was full of these kinds of education opportunities.

"Do your twenty years, get your pension, get out and finish your degree or community college certificate," I told them. "In other words, use your degree, or certificate, to start yourself on a lucrative career."

One old Warrant Officer took exception to my speech. He implied that the gist of my speech was that anyone who spent more than twenty years in the military was not the brightest bulb on the tree. I concurred.. He met me alone in the parking lot. He was steamed and said, "I should clean your clock."

"Good", I thought, "no witnesses."

I took that weasel up on his challenge, and dared him. I figured that physically, an old man like him wasn't up to the challenge..

"You'd better clear out, or I'm going to kick your ass," I said.

He left the parking lot and, needless to say, I left the speaking club. There was no rank involved, as long as you agreed with the martinets. That lesson stood me in good stead later on.

Ottawa was an expensive place to live. Margaret got a part-time job cleaning offices, at the International Airport. She, and our neighbour, Elizabeth, worked there together. Elizabeth was a peach. She liked shoveling snow but her husband Paul, didn't. She would tap, tap, tap on my window and say, "Now sir, let's get it done." Out I would go. She wanted to shovel even in a blizzard. We would get the sidewalk steps shoveled off just in time to start all over again. It was good fun to work together.

I sold Elizabeth an old bike, with a broken frame. I put some masking tape over it to hide the break. One day, she came back madder than a hatter. The bike was in two pieces. I laughed, and said buyer beware. I should have listened to myself. I bought an old chesterfield from her. I went to set it up, and it only had three legs. She said, "Now we are even." We still stay in touch forty some years later. Liz dropped in about two days after I wrote this – she remembered every detail of me being a good neighbour.

Kids used to ride their bikes to the end of the sidewalk, over my lawn, and down the hill. They thought it was great fun but it was damaging the lawn. One night I strung a clothesline across the width of the lawn and waited. Sper-rang!! It was like a slingshot. That was the end of them riding on my lawn.

Years earlier, Marg was cleaning offices at the airport. One of her foremen was Lou. He was a joker. He used to say, "What? Me worry?" He was a riot to be around. One day, he showed up with a little black, and white, kitten with a red ribbon around its neck. Lou even supplied a food dish. Marg, and Carol Ann, fell in love with that damn cat. I put on an act that I could barely tolerate him, but really, I thought the world of that cat.

When he was older, he climbed the brick wall of our PMQ bungalow. A dog was after him. Boots was able to hang there until we chased the dog away. He was sure glad to slide to the ground. Marg was standing on a chair, at our open kitchen door, while the cat was being chased round, and round her chair by the neighbour's dog. The neighbour was a Major.

"Get out of here right now!" Marg screamed. She was yelling at the dog. The poor Major, whom she hadn't noticed, pleaded, "But madam, I only want my dog!" He was a great neighbor, and a really decent officer.

We had an air force golf course at Uplands where the enlisted ranks got subsidized rates. Bob Legault, and I, worked midnights and did a lot of golfing in the summer. I got my first set of clubs at Giant Tiger, in Ottawa, including all the odd numbered irons, and a couple of woods.

Bob had a huge old black Buick. Our cat, Boots, would constantly run in front of his car. Bob teased Marg by saying, "Here come da Big Black Judge. He's going to get Boots." Needless to say he managed to avoid Boots who lived to be seventeen.

I had a Canadian Tire Credit Card. Bob did not. I would put parts for his old Buick on my card, and he would pay me. He never took me for a nickel but when I got the cash, I would pay the minimum payment and the extra money would vaporize. You know how that goes! Welcome to Economics 101. That lesson stuck with me forever. Don't run a balance on a credit card. Pay it off. After that, we always did.

We had a Fuller Brush Man (a door-to-door peddler) on the base. He handled cleaning agents, hair brushes, tonics and cosmetics. He was transferred, and told me I should take a shot at it. I said, "Why not?" It was part-time with flexible hours. I became a Section Manager with Fuller Brush, and was responsible for 2,000 houses. I offered part-time selling positions to the guys I worked with, as well as their spouses. It worked out to about 400 houses per salesperson. I was making good part-time money, and so were my salespeople. A couple of them got promoted in the air force. This proved awkward since they became my bosses in the military, and I was still their boss in Fuller Brush.

That rank structure really sucked for me. It caused an awkward flare-up. Before this situation, three of us had bought adjoining lots on the Ottawa River. Lloyd was from Pembroke, and knew the area. We had beachfront on Allumette Island, Quebec. It had a beautiful, sandy beach, shady maple trees towards the back of the lot. The Ottawa River was so wide, they called it Lake Victoria. The water was sparkling and clean. What a paradise! We enjoyed this beautiful space every summer as it was just one hundred miles from our home in Ottawa.

We bought the property from an old farmer, and his French-Canadian wife. I was dickering with him. He let me put $400 down, which I had borrowed. When I had paid the down payment off, I borrowed another $600 so that the property was paid in full.

Marg and I were playing bridge with the farmer's wife, Vi, in the late fall. The snow was really pretty but it would get dark so quickly. As we were playing cards, the time went flying, and we didn't notice that the snow was piling up. We headed back to Ottawa in a foot of snow. It was pretty, but daunting.

In the spring, logging companies would run logs down the river. They had big log booms pulled by a tugboat. (A log boom is a floating fence of logs that is chained together to corral the loose logs being guided down the river.) This must have been one of the last places in Canada to move logs in this way. Their crews had the right to retrieve their logs from your property, after the spring floods. There was a legal 'High Water Mark' which indicated the highest level on the shore that the water reached in a 100 year period that might capture the loose logs. The logs were all stamped. They did not take lightly to people sawing the ends off their logs, thus removing the stamped markings. You had better make sure the evidence was the first to go in the fire!

I bought an old construction trailer for $400. It had a propane kitchen stove, an old refrigerator, one room, and too many mice. Our old cat, Boots, caught ONE and then retired. The mouse traps had to do the rest. In the middle of the night, SNAP, the trap tripped. Most of the time, it was the cat eating the cheese bait that sprung the trap. He must have had a perpetual headache.

Marg was afraid her precious cat would get lost in the backwoods. I was afraid he wouldn't. We put him on a leash. He always went with us to the trailer. The car broke down, naturally. The cat was on the leash but he wouldn't walk on the gravel road. I had to carry our over-weight, huge, Boots for over a mile.

I had trouble getting the lawyer to physically hand me my deed. I suspected Quebec Law might be a lot different than Ontario Law. His secretary privately said I should get in touch with the Quebec equivalent of the Ontario Bar Association. She said she would pass the word to the lawyer of my intentions. I was there when he was scurrying around the office. At first I thought he was crooked. Nope, just stupid, because he finally found my deed on the windowsill where he had left it.

We got our electrical service wired to a pole on our beach lot. It cost $100 which was quite a bargain. The extension cord had two male plugs! One went to the pole, and the other to the female receptacle on the trailer. I had never had a shock from grabbing a male plug by the prongs, until then. This time, I found out I was getting the jolt from the source! I learned eventually, after about three jolts, that I'd better plug the trailer in first.

The farmer's son took my daughter, Carol Ann, and I out on his sailboat. It was a thrilling ride, as it cut through the water. I wasn't much of a boat person, but after feeling that thrill, I borrowed a 12-foot boat with a small motor. Carol Ann, and I were motoring along, when it happened. We hit some hidden pilings from an old dock. What a noise! We came ashore in a hurry. My daughter never got in a small boat again. This was immediately after we had been on a B.C. Ferry from Vancouver to Victoria. The ferry had to swerve as hard as it could to miss a cattle boat. Carol Ann was right beside the whistle. Between the sudden movement, and the noise from the fog horn, she was one terrified little girl!

My part-time Fuller Brush business was a success. I have two silver plaques for the best sales in Ottawa. Not too shabby. My work force, however, had had enough. Their wives had good jobs so the monetary incentive was no longer there. I could see this coming. They quit 'en masse', which felt like a revolt to me. Little did they know a friend of mine, and myself, could look after their houses. I had complete records of sales.

Bill and I just serviced the houses with previous sales except for the P.M.Q.'s as new tenants were always posted in. We called on every one of them. Bill gave his customers a great deal on scented candles. The company promotion assured us the price was the lowest in Canada. Bill promoted them, and sold a bunch. K-Mart undercut him. His customers were livid! He did the right thing, and gave them two dollars off their next purchase. They were happy, and he kept his customers.

I think every Canadian should attend the Remembrance Day Ceremony, in Ottawa, at least once in their lifetime. We attended with our daughter, Carol Ann. The television coverage is good but the somber, soulful mood can only be captured by being there. You will walk away with a sense of awe for the sacrifices made by our brave men, and women.

Sometimes, I would help Marg clean offices at a government building. Her cleaning company was happy with that arrangement. They would get four man-hours of work from us and pay for three. She would be finished one hour earlier, and they saved one hour in wages. It was win-win.

Smoking was still in, and very big. Our hands, and clothes, would reek of tobacco. Each desk had a large, round, amber, glass ashtray. Did these people ever work? Each ashtray was filled to the brim. We emptied, and washed, each one.

Marg was still shy. We had to pass through the building basement on our way to the offices. Quantities of empty filing cabinets, covered with dust, were stored there. For some reason known only to her, she felt impish. She used her finger to write in the dust.

"I am dirty, wash me." She was dumbstruck the next evening to see a reply,

"I am dirty too, bleep me." That was the end of Marg's writing career.

Our old 1963 vintage Mercury did not like Ottawa's frigid winters. After each cleaning session, we would cross our fingers. Barely turning over, the old Merc would moan and groan. Thank goodness, she always fired up, and never stranded us. The parking lot was deserted at that time of night, and we could have ill-afforded the "jump" from C.A.A.

My daughter decided she wanted to play softball. She looked cute in her ball uniform. The only snag was, you guessed it; there was no coach. So, I volunteered. I told the girls that I knew very little about softball, even though I agreed to coach. Carol Ann was no ball player, and I was no coach, but we had fun. I said to her, "I know little girls cry easily so please don't."

I guess the air force knew I was contented in Ottawa. I had a decent income, enjoyed our beautiful summer place, and life was good – too good. So I was transferred. We had lots of notice as the whole squadron of Hercules aircraft, and personnel, were transferred at the same time. Naturally, the Hercules flight simulator, and personnel transferred, also.

Before our departure, Marg flew to B.C. to visit her sister. Carol Ann, and I, batched it for two weeks. She was too young to do much cooking. I was too dim to try it. We ate a lot of Kraft Dinner and had lots of unique travel experiences. We saw the Auto Museum in Oshawa. Carol Ann put up with it. I showed her a buffalo herd, in a large fenced-in field, and that was more to her liking. As we were standing in line, to see deer at the Bowmanville Zoo, this nasty, old woman flew at me out of nowhere.

"Are you calling me an old crow?"

She repeated the question several times! For once in my life, I was speechless. My daughter was totally upset. I can't remember if she was crying but, because of Carol Ann's state, I told the woman, "Of course I didn't call you an old crow."

Then we heard it for the first time.

"Watch it, you old crow, you old crow, you old crow."

The culprit was a real live black-feathered talking crow. I don't know the age of that bird but he sure could land a person in a lot of trouble. I accepted the woman's apologies. No harm done.

Marg couldn't wait to relay her misadventures to us. Her brother-in-law's car broke down, miles from the Victoria Airport, while she was trying to connect for her flight back. Marg must have been very anxious to see us because she accepted a ride from some mature hippies. They took a short-cut onto a B.C. Ferry, and reached the airport just in time for Marg to scramble abroad. My good wife doesn't drink but, she confessed, she had two large glasses of wine after she was airborne.

Just before our transfer to Trenton, we revisited two unique bars on Allumette Island. We had a saying in Quebec: "If you were big enough to crawl onto a bar stool, you were old enough to drink!" Times do change. Fred's Place was run by an ex-cop with the Quebec Provincial Police. He put up with no shenanigans but you could have a good time there. Anyone could haul their instruments in, and have a jam session. The closing time was flexible.

Sikorsky's Bar hit the papers because more than one person saw flying saucers, or UFO's, there. I was down at the river, one dark night, and I saw flashing lights. They were too high to be on a boat. I was beginning to believe in UFO's myself when the mystery was solved. A float plane was 'taxing' up the river in the middle of the night. We ever heard any more about it, but I doubt it would have taken off in the dark of the night. One wooden log, and they would be history. UFO's -- my foot.

Chapter Twelve

Hitting the Books for a New Career

My old running mate, Bob, found it hard to find affordable housing in Trenton when he was transferred there, before the rest of us. I used to drive him to catch his air force flight from the International Ottawa Terminal. One day, we were in the lounge having a few beers before his flight. Time flew, and the boarding time came, and went. Just when we saw the ground crew pulling the portable loading ramp away, Bob took off like a shot. I think he got crap from everyone from the stewardess, to the pilot. Having no rank stinks. They really roasted him!

Imagine the rush to acquire housing for hundreds of families descending on the town of Trenton, Ontario all at the same time. The higher ranks and high income personnel could buy homes, albeit at inflated, bloated, real estate prices. The law of supply and demand kicked into high gear. No supply – high demand. Many guys were put up in Trenton barracks while their families were stuck in Ottawa.

You sure found out how to look after yourself, as the 'help' network in the air force was sorely missing. I knew of a technician in Trenton who was being transferred to Lahr, Germany. Months earlier – through the rumour mill, I had hatched a tentative plan with him. If his transfer came to fruition, and if I was transferred to Trenton, then I would rent his house. Being an absentee landlord across the Atlantic Ocean is not ideal. With all the 'ifs' out of the way, we moved into his old war-time frame house, just as smooth as silk. Carol Ann, and I, loved it. Marg, not so much.

The first night we were there, we saw a skunk saunter up the driveway, and disappear under our house. We were worried because these old places had no basements. We caught a whiff of if for a few days, and then it disappeared.

I couldn't take a chance in sealing off the floor grate. What if he was still in there, or there some other rodent? Originally, they had a floor furnace with a steel grate, as part of your living room floor. But the owners decided to remove the furnace, and leave the hole with a sturdy grate covering the floor.

We heard a commotion, and our cat started meowing. At first, we thought he had found a skunk, but there was no stench. We opened the grate, and somehow, 'that damn cat' Boots had found a long haired, gray cat. The mysterious gray cat was still a kitten. So guess who ended up with two damn cats!

Usually, personality clashes didn't last too long in the air force. One or the other of the culprits usually got transferred. However, when you've worked with the same dozen people, and a few IDIOTS for five years, it gets irksome. When you are all transferred en masse to a new base, within the confines of the simulator trade, it becomes impossible to be separated. This is especially true when you are on the bottom of the pecking order. I was the bottom.

As I described in my speech in 1966, I was working toward my twenty year pension, while pursuing my education. I jumped from Grade Ten to Grade Thirteen. (I had this option as I was an 'adult learner'.) I was also given lots of bad advice. I think the advice was to take one step at a time. If I had followed that advice, I would virtually be an old man by the time I completed Grade Thirteen. For me, time was of the essence, yet I felt I was constantly being hassled.

While in Ottawa, we all made sure that other crew-mates got to go to university, by helping them by working extra shifts for them. I thought it was my turn for some consideration. I took summer school during my leave, and I took Grade Thirteen English through correspondence courses.

I often took individual days of leave when my inconsiderate bosses didn't want to give me three hours off on an evening shift. This happened only once every three weeks. We worked days, evenings, and midnights.

The crunch came when I had one more subject for Grade Thirteen to be completed. My boss decided that his version of fair was to let another technician have an educational opportunity. The only trouble was that they rigged the other guy's course to fall on the same night as my compulsory course. I needed just this one compulsory course to complete my Grade Thirteen, while the other 'scholar" required twenty-seven courses, and could have scheduled any other night.

I did not take this new very well. While socializing with the boss, over a few beers, I hit the roof. We had a little together time – one on one, no witnesses. I told the Sergeant that I would take a day's leave instead of trying to get the time off. He said I couldn't do it. I said that he couldn't stop me, and that I would go over his head. Unfortunately, his immediate supervisor was cut with the same cloth as the Sergeant. No luck there!

I saw the individual 'wanna be' student. We were the same rank, and I unloaded on him. He was a boozer, and decided the twenty-seven courses would eat into his drinking time. Luckily, the boozer gave up his quest for a higher education. I really think the Sergeant had instigated the whole thing.

Things were pretty dire for me. I strove to do my job as well as possible. I felt like I was on somebody's hit list.

Before my final course, I had the good fortune to be in charge of our modification section. One young technician came away from our test bench with half a screwdriver shaft burned off, and a glazed look in his eyes. He was okay, but had been scared almost to death. He should have known better. Our safety procedures were pretty strict. However, the test bench wasn't idiot proof, and we discovered there was a design fault in it. I drew up a modification, and drafted it all out. (I was ready to submit it when I got back from a week's leave. I didn't travel anywhere and my leave pass destination attested to this fact.)

These modifications could result in a cash grant, or an 'atta boy' letter. My phone rang at home.

"Ken, you know that modification you designed and worked on?" Bill asked. "Your boss is going to sign his name to it and take all the credit."

I was in our section in twenty minutes wanting a clarification of what amounted to fraud.

"I didn't want to bother you when you were on leave," said the boss. "I thought I would sign it and clear out some paperwork. You're here now so I guess you may as well sign it yourself."

It was really big of him, I thought.

It turned out to be a good safety modification, no cash award, but I had the satisfaction of making things a little safer for our personnel.

Chapter Thirteen

Legal Headaches of Home and Property Ownership

When I was working days, my previous summer school course was covered by my leave. Grade Thirteen Calculus was no joke. I was missing Grades Eleven, and Twelve, math, but our air force simulator specialty courses filled in some of the gaps. Another airman, and myself, were having a hard time of it.

A twenty-year-old girl was taking the course for the second time. She had passed it already but wanted to improve her mark for university acceptance. She offered to tutor both of us. We would sit around my kitchen table, and she would drill us on the lesson that we had just covered, and preview the next day's lesson. It took the mystery out of Calculus. I'm sure she made an excellent math teacher.

Every week my classmates, Wally and Ester, and I would be in a Grade Thirteen Biology course. When I put a worm in the skeleton's mouth, the teacher did not appreciate it. Another time, we had to dissect a fetal piglet. It stank of preservative. Poor Ester had a hard time of it.

During this tumultuous time, we were able to buy our first house thanks to a new provincial government subsidized housing program. There was a catch. There was a maximum you could earn to qualify. You can bet every corporal in the forces was making a poor enough income to buy one of the houses. Under the program, you bought the house, and leased the land. (The government would later offer the land to the homeowner.) Most of us bought the land, to offset any problems that could arise when listing it for re-sale.

I also delved into the land speculation market. The NDP Government, in British Columbia, was making vague nationalist threats aimed at American land speculators. No one knew if those threats were also aimed at Canadians from other provinces. I figured I would buy in BC, and then, regardless of politics I would have 'Squatters Rights', so to speak. My sister lived in Smithers, BC, which was between Prince George and Prince Rupert, and way out in the sticks. Her husband worked out of Smithers, on the railroad.

Gayle lined up a lawyer to represent me in case I found some land that I was interested in. I found four-and-a-half acres on Hudson Bay Mountain. It was the last piece of private land before it turned into Crown land, the glacier, the mountain range and the Pacific Ocean. Everything went without a hitch, with the realtor, and the lawyer, until I tried to sell it years later. The lady real estate agent who I retained to list the property, made one phone call. She came back, saying she couldn't handle my listing as I had no legal right-of-way. Shocking! What? Apparently there was no fraud; just massive incompetence! Both the original lawyer, and the original realtor for the vendor, should have spotted this error. That's small town BC, for you. I was stonewalled at every junction!

Living in Ontario, and trying to straighten out this mess in BC, wasn't working. We travelled to BC on money we could ill-afford. My original lawyer had been promoted to judge, and had left town. The original realtor had since quit, and I don't know why! Get this! I had a road into my place but it wasn't mine. My new realtor would list my land if I could get legal right-of-way. She knew who owned the land, the person I needed to secure legal right-of-way, and she said she would visit him. I would be guaranteed my listing if we could resolve this glitch – this mighty Big Glitch.

The rancher who owned the property I needed hated women. My female representative was sent packing. The story was that his wife had left town with her lesbian lover.

I had no choice; I would have to pay him a visit. This wasn't easy because he had a huge dog chained by his sidewalk. I managed to get by the do, who was straining at his chain, just out of man-eating range. I got some courage from somewhere. Some people would say it was desperation.

I knocked at the door. Right. Nobody home. I walked a very intimidating line past that ferocious dog back to my car. I repeated the tightrope act that evening. Cutting to the chase, the rancher knew why I was there.

"Make me an offer," he said.

I told him I knew he had me between a rock and a hard place. We decided he would get the land appraised, and we would go from there. He phone me, all excited. He quoted me what they said it was worth, saying that it was too much money. How about half? He knew I had to have the land, and was still willing to charge me half the appraised value, which was pretty good. We made a legal deal very quickly, and I thanked him profusely.

Chapter Fourteen

Goodbye Air Force - Hello 'Civvy' Street

We had a thorough inspection of our air force simulator section. The engineering officer was totally impressed with the way the Projects and Modifications Department was being handled. I was in charge of that department, and won a deserving airman's trip to South America.

My assessment review, by my Sergeant, would have been marginal. In a session with my Sergeant's superior, the Warrant Officer told me that they would make my review score quite low and improve it each time. This would show that I was making real progress towards promotion.

Actually they both did it to make themselves look good, as I was supposedly under their guidance. They were 'grooming' me. What a pair of sick souls!

I continued to follow my own advice, as set out in my old speech of 1966, and I completed my Grade Thirteen, in 1977. I wanted to leave the air force as quickly as possible but I had to put in for my release one year in advance. There were two conditions for this. First, I couldn't put in for a transfer as it would not be feasible for the air force to relocate me with less than a year to go. Secondly, there would also be no promotion (Haha).

I was pretty jaded, to say the least, and was assigned every 'Joe job' available. One time, they needed people to drive trucks for the transport section. We usually drew names, or cut cards, for all these nuisance jobs. Not this time – I was it!

Driving trucks is about as far from fixing analog, and digital, flight simulators as you can get. The Sergeant, who was giving us the driving test which was mandatory before driving those trucks, thought we might fail the test on purpose. We told him not to be so bloody stupid. One man out of the five of us had ripped the side mirror off the van on his driver test. He was returned to his normal duties. As for the rest of us, we toughed it out.

My eye glasses got mysteriously crushed. He ordered me to drive anyway! I told him to put it in writing, as I was 'visually restricted to glasses' on my Ontario driver's license. I won my argument, but it didn't matter; the new glasses were there in a day or two.

We also kept 'forgetting' to wash our trucks. This caused the dispatcher a lot of heartburn. These bozos didn't want to give us the same amount of time off for lunch as their regular drivers. We soon got that straightened out. One other thing that drove them crazy was our waiting for clearance from the tower to cross the runways. We milked that plenty! I finally had done my penance, and was returned to the simulator section.

Wally, my old classmate, and I, were working the midnight shift. He was intelligent, quiet and very private. In spite of this we worked well together. We did a virtual ton of inspection cards on our shift. A guideline was provided as far as allocation was concerned. The Warrant Officer scanned a huge deck of work cards we had completed when he arrived at 8 a.m. He then curtly ordered us back to the computer room. He had us stand at attention, and started to berate us, saying, "You must have signed out all the cards and drank coffee all night."

What he, and his 'yes-sir' Sergeant neglected to do, was to view the individual time allocated for each task. I usually kept my mouth shut in front of witnesses. He clasped his hands behind his back, paced back and forth, and kept looking at the wall. That was it.

"Is there a message on that wall, Warrant?" I asked. He got red in the face and went ballistic.

"There's a message there alright," he snarled. We, the two criminals, the Sergeant and the old Warrant Officer, went through the cards and found out that everything was done right. Oh yes! An apology did NOT come from either one of the 'Boobsy' twins.

The air force was aligning our trade with an aircraft trade. My illustrious bosses said it would never work. They were right, of course. They sent me over to the hangar line, fully expecting me to prove that the two trades were completely incompatible. However, I had ten years as an aircraft electrician, and promptly told my new bosses that I would be the best integrated systems technician that they had ever seen.

About a week after peppering everyone with trade questions, going over wiring and maintenance procedures, they knew I meant it. I was again misemployed.

My old Warrant Officer phoned me at home.

"Guess who would have gotten promoted if his release wasn't in?" he asked.

"Stick it," I said.

"That's what I expected," came the reply.

I wanted that promotion, so I phoned back to that same Warrant Officer, and said I wanted to cancel my release to gain my promotion. The Warrant got me an interview with a Captain. I told him that I thought jobs had dried up, and I'd probably stay in for another few years. My release was cancelled, and I became a proud Master Corporal. As soon as it was official, I put my release in, once again, for as soon as possible. There were a lot of ruffled feathers over that deal. As you have probably sensed by now, my work was good but my attitude stank.

We had a promotion tradition. The guy who got promoted would buy a case of beer. After work, we'd have a few beer in the section, to celebrate his good fortune. The tradition changed for me. They forbade this practice as far as I was concerned.

Before my release, I found the education officer. We actually had one! None of us seemed to know about it. He gave me a big spiel about Project Loyalist, at Loyalist College, in Belleville, Ontario. On the surface, it looked like the air force was partnering with them, and sharing the funding cost.

I was now out of the forces and job security was a thing of the past. I enrolled into Loyalist College, which gave me two months off in the summer, before the course started.

I had upgraded my education while working full time and we had saved enough money, from my rehabilitation leave, to finance my post-secondary education. My wife's income really helped. Don't ever under-estimate the encouragement, and support, of a good wife. She can make or break your dreams. Marg supported my dreams the whole way.

Ironically, I received a Canadian Decoration Medal for meritorious service! We airmen referred to it as twelve years of undetected crime.

Marg took this 'Civilian' (Me) with her to Niagara Falls for her Union Convention 1977. I celebrated my new freedom.

Chapter Fifteen

Community College - Here I Come!

I had a couple of months leave before starting my two-year electronic engineering technician's course. I spent my time off with my 'new-to-me' 100-cc trail/street motorcycle. I put hundreds of miles on it in a very short time. It was a blast. I was careening through old railway yards, and dodging cops, on their routine patrols. That was part of the fun.

I could go cross-country, through an abandoned apple orchard which bordered on my back yard. I felt so free. I was under the assumption that the air force was funding my engineering course; I soon learned not to assume anything. An ex-navy man was one of my classmates. We just happened to hit it off. Our first paycheque was in our school mail slots. We opened them at the same time.

I said to Red, "What the bleep is this?" I asked Red. "Are you unemployed?" "No bloody way!" he responded.

Then Red asked me the same question. Same answer – No.

Both of our cheques were from the Unemployment Insurance Commission! The military force had 'snowed' us again! We both thought the military was footing the bill for our education. I suppose they never in 'black and white' stated that, but they never denied it, either. Neither Red, nor, I had ever been unemployed in our lives, but, practicality-speaking, getting the UI cheque made us happy -- after we got over our shock. After our mutual embarrassment, we never mentioned the cheques again. In retrospect, the military did do us one service. They typed out twenty resumes for each of us, -- one for each year of service. They really knocked themselves out!

Our two-year course was crammed into one year. Apparently, this was done to fit in with the Unemployment Insurance funding guidelines. We had a very mixed bag of students. Some were there just to collect their UI cheques. We had twelve younger students who had no military background and five ex-non-commissioned officers. (The NCOs had been my nemeses for the full twenty years of military service.) The workload was enormous.

Our senior instructor was brilliant, and a taskmaster. He had an award on his wall in his office for the highest mark in Calculus at Queen's University, up to that point. He told us to form study groups, and refrain from letting a few lazy individuals copy our homework, or try to hitch a free ride. After working our tails off, we very quickly cut the free-loaders out of the four study groups. I must note, with some satisfaction, that not one ex-NCO was standing on the platform with us on graduation day.

For years, I had thought that only four of us had graduated out of the twenty-four, but according to our graduation program, five of us had actually succeeded. One fellow took a job immediately and had his diploma mailed to him. This meant that there were nineteen students who didn't achieve the objectives in the allotted time. Many just drifted away. Some figured they'd do their technical report later, and then receive their diploma. For me, I knew it was now, or never. I burned the midnight oil, and apparently, so did a few others.

Our group included a bright kid named Steve. He was smart, had his Grade Thirteen, but had no electronic background. Red, and I, tutored him, and showed him the practical aspects of the course. It was a good thing Steve was a fast learner. He is still in Belleville, and I will be in touch with him, in the near future.

We were having a practical exam on the oscilloscope and Steve thought he needed more practice. The scope was old hat to me. We were allowed to work in the labs at night, but we had to sign in with a Commissionaire. In those days, all Commissionaires were ex-military, and most were ex-NCOs, with an attitude. The one on duty was trying to give us a hard time. I unloaded on him. I told him we weren't still in the military, and that he also had a boss. Miraculously, the key appeared.

Steve passed the practical exam on a breeze. After that, he called me Professor Kenny.

Our Friday night study sessions, invariably, ended up at Mother's Restaurant, in Belleville. A few of us drank too much wine just to unwind. The waitresses were dressed in 19ᵗʰ Century period costumes with long dresses and fancy hats. Our study group usually ordered lots of spaghetti, and meat balls. The waitresses would tie long bibs around our necks from behind us. We had great fun leaning our heads back as far as we could!

Our favourite waitress was a well-built blonde. Her cap covered most of her hair but we all agreed she was a blonde! (More about this blonde later.)

We studied every night. One Sunday afternoon, Red mixed a quart of cocktails, and we found a picnic table in the park, ready to hit the books. We also hit the booze, and decided we had studied enough. I picked up my wife, Marg, and we all went for Chinese food. Red somehow broke a chair in the basement, so we cleared out in a hurry, as our bill had already been paid.

As a side note: In 2012, I started walking in the park that borders on the Bay of Quinte. I ran into a fellow classmate from Loyalist. He was twenty years younger than me, and he recognized me at once, probably from my voice. He had completed his last outstanding assignment from Loyalist a year after he graduated. It was the mandatory technical report. He received his diploma, and landed a great job in Belleville.

Never give up. It worked for him.

Graduation was such sweet success!

The 'unlikely graduate' never gave up. 1979 Graduation from Loyalist College in Belleville, Ontario as an Electronic Engineering Technician.

Chapter Sixteen

Teachers' College at Queen's University

I had one more hurdle to clear – Teachers' College! I submitted my resume, and application to Queen's University. I wanted to attend Duncan MacArthur Hall. After attending Loyalist, I was no longer as intimidated with higher education. I found out that there were great professors, and not-so-great professors.

I was readily accepted into the Electronics Teaching Program. We had six hours of theory tests, and six hours of practical tests, before we could be accepted. The first day of school was general indoctrination for all candidates, regardless of subject specialty. As you probably know, there are many subjects, and programs, to be taught in Ontario's teaching curricula.

I was standing alone, feeling very lost, when a statuesque blonde embraced me in a wonderful bear hug. I was so shocked that I didn't reciprocate.

"You don't recognize me, do you?" she said, backing off, in a huff.

"I wish I did," I said.

She quickly informed me that under all those layers of Mother's Restaurant clothing, she was indeed that striking blonde who had been our waitress for the last year! She was majoring in physical education. She informed me that both she, and her girlfriend, were going through to be English teachers, and said they could use a ride from Belleville to Duncan MacArthur, in Kingston.

I had a few reservations about car-pooling, but those reservations quickly dissipated. Each girl would pick up 50 per cent of the cost of the gas. Their husbands were working, and I wasn't.

Her girlfriend was a little older, and was going to be a top-notch English teacher. Our car-pooling worked out perfectly. I never had to wait once for them during that whole school year.

Practice teaching rounds, in real high schools, were the highlights of our course. We would tell each other all the stories about our students. A few of us had some misadventures that we also 'fessed up to.

Most of our teacher supervisors were encouraging, and helpful. However, one thought that the student English teacher was her private secretary. She had her performing all the mundane tasks that a teacher does, but none of the teaching. The whole idea of these placements was to give the student teachers instruction time in a classroom. Apparently, that veteran teacher had put all these mundane tasks on student teachers for years.

Sandra, the student English teacher, had had enough, and wrote a formal complaint to the Dean. That veteran teacher never had a placement student teacher, again. Thankfully, that teacher was the exception and not the rule.

All technical teachers had to complete a major project called Project Design. Its aim was to test our flexibility, our willingness to participate in group work, and our ability to invent new concepts. Above all, we had to turn out a new product in a collaborative, problem-solving manner. The product had to be more inexpensive, more durable than the original ones, and aesthetic to the eyes.

Five would-be technical teachers were assigned by our faculty to form our consortium. The faculty dictated that it had to consist of a variety of trades and skills. We had a carpenter, machinist, auto-mechanic, boatbuilder, and 'last and least', ME, the electronics teacher. (To clarify my qualifications, I graduated to teach Grades Nine and Ten for electricity, and all Grades Nine, to Twelve, for electronics.)

Our professor let it slip that working on this kind of project would, and could, cause dissension and disarray within our consortium. We solved that problem. Our consortium voted on everything, agreeing that decisions of the majority ruled. The reason our team was successful probably had to do with the fact that each of us had come through the school of hard knocks. As mature students, we had all dealt with families, coworkers, bosses, customers and clients at one time, or another.

Luck, not design, had made the five of us, who were assigned to our consortium, into a cohesive group.

The first part of our project involved selecting a subject item. Ours fell into our lap. Peter, our machinist, was also a first-class kayak paddler. He had qualified for the 1980 Olympics, shortly before our 1979 Teachers' Course.

(Our professor's pet project was converting an old Datsun into an electric car. I knew that, with my background in electricity and electronics, I would be over-ruled by the prof's opinions, as he was an electrical engineer. No thanks!)

We kicked some other ideas around, but Peter lamented about the air carrier's care – or lack of care – of his two paddles. Peter was far from rich, and Olympic grants were practically unheard of, in 1979. In the pre-Olympic trials, he had to travel by air. His paddles would arrive with their blades split or broken. Repair costs were steep, but the cessation of training was the real fallout until his equipment would be repaired. He continually had to borrow some inferior paddles to make do until repairs were carried out. This was a real challenge!

We decided, by consensus, that designing a new type kayak paddle would be our project. All of our paperwork, and proposals, were accepted.

Our boat builder, who had extensive experience with fibreglass, jumped at the chance to tell us about a relatively new material called Kevlar. That was the key word – NEW. It was being used for bullet-proof vests for the police forces, and was originally designed to replace the steel belts in automobile tires.

Our research on Kevlar supported our idea that it would be ideal for 'Peter's Paddle,' as our project was named. Kevlar was four times as strong as steel, so we knew that our finished project would exceed all the stringent requirements.

While we attended psychology classes, and speaking classes, the majority of our time was spent on our Project Design endeavour. It seemed to us that our professor was a little perplexed about the harmony we exhibited within our group. He offered to help remove any roadblocks, or solve very difficult problems that he was sure we would encounter. Surprise! We had none – personally or professionally.

Peter, our leader, then dropped a bomb on us. He said we were now 'up the creek without a paddle' – 'Peter's Paddle' that is. Queen's University, in its wisdom, decided that because we were using their shop equipment, that the paddle was going to be theirs, upon completion. They wanted our patent rights! If the paddle was successful in the Olympics, Queen's would have gained world-wide recognition and lots of prestige. We were steamed! We had overcome insurmountable odds to become Ontario High School Teachers, and we were losing our personal recognition for the project.

We had a private strategy meeting without Peter. All four of us decided, without question, what to do. We signed present and future rights, revenues and royalties, over to Peter. After all, the paddle was his idea, and he would be representing Canada in the 1980 Games. We felt he deserved the recognition, and financial rewards, if any were generated. The professor should have given us top marks for the problem-solving portion of Project Design. We told him that Peter owned the patent rights and that was that! Our boat-builder said that we could use HIS equipment for the molds, and anything else we needed. He still had industrial contacts for materials, and advice from the boat-building community.

Peter's Paddle - Made from the new miracle material,
Kevlar – it became the amazing Kevlar Kayak Paddle.

The practice-teaching sessions were a welcome interlude. We were away from the artificial university world, and were now nose-to-nose with the kids. Because I had a knack for showing new technicians around in the air force, I was well prepared for the teaching tasks ahead. A few problems always appeared, of course

Vacuum tube electronics were rapidly being replaced by solid-state advances. Some schools had not yet made the transition. I let it slip, to my supervising teacher, that his vacuum tube equipment was redundant. Big mistake. I still hadn't learned to shut my mouth! He informed me abruptly, that I'd better get reacquainted with tubes in a hurry. I did my best to pacify his hurt feelings. After all, he was writing up my teaching evaluation. Although my two-year electronic engineering technician course taught me lots of theory, it didn't teach me 'tact'. I was a little hard-pressed, but I learned to mellow after that. Because I worked well with kids, the majority of my reports were top of the mark!

The Teachers' College offered us a choice for one of our longer practice placements. I was very wary, after my air force experiences with transfers, to agree to locations that were not my choices. (Remember, the time when if I wanted a military transfer to BC, they would ensure I ended up in Nova Scotia.)

I told the Teachers' College to place me wherever they wanted. They were somewhat taken aback, and assured me they would listen to, and accommodate, each one of us. I asked for Trenton because I lived there. It was Déjà Vu, all over again. I was placed at the outer limits of their catchment area. Yes! I was off to Ottawa – expensive Ottawa at that!

By this time, problem-solving had become routine to me. I called up an old simulator technician in Ottawa. Smokey had just retired before we moved the squadron to CFB Trenton. I had helped him with his move into his home, and we got along just fine. He said the timing was perfect, as his wife would be in Germany, and he was 'baching' it. He had a big, old house on one of the downtown side streets. He had no car, and it didn't occur to him to mention that he had no driveway. I guess he thought I could park on the street. Every morning, I had a parking ticket! Guess it was still cheaper than a motel room. The first day of practice teaching, I had a flat tire. I left early enough so that I could change the tire, and get cleaned up without being late. The placement was a rewarding experience, and before I knew it, I was back at Teachers' College.

There was one candidate who should never have chosen teaching as a career. His name was Frank something, or other. I do know that his last name started with a 'U'. He was a nasty, obnoxious little man. Our consortium called him 'F' 'U'.

Each time the college suggested he leave, he would threaten to sue. He didn't drop the course until his final failing mark. I had the misfortune of doing a practice placement after 'F' 'U' had been practising at that class.

The Grade Nine kids finally confided in me about an experience they had with Frank. At this point, the kids knew very little about electricity. However, they procured a red jumper cable, and a black jumper cable, with no power attached. When Frank came in the door, they slammed the black clip and the red clip together. In unison, they yelled 'BANG'!

Poor Frank pretty well jumped out of his skin. They each got a week's detention, but told me that it was worth it. The system works. He never became a teacher.

Another project, that we were responsible for, was a Community Services Project. This time, the college accepted our choices, and we could arrange our own placements. This fit me like a glove. I opted for Loyalist College, in Belleville. I was a graduate the year before, and they were delighted to accommodate me.

Our Teachers' College was located across the road from the Women's Federal Prison in Kingston. Two of our younger candidates decided they would tutor some of these women in the field of basic education. I think the student teachers got the education. These prisoners were tough, and worldly, and probably they thought time would pass more quickly if they could embarrass these younger student teachers. Once the teachers opted in, there was no opting out. Watch what you volunteer for.

One time in college, I thought I had done a cracker jack job on an essay. However, I received a very low mark. I went to the professor's office, and talked to the receptionist, saying, "I want to see the jack-ass who marked my paper."

I knew that professors did very little marking on their own. There was an awkward silence. I had found the 'jack-ass'. While she didn't admit it, once she had regained her composure, she assured me the professor would see my essay for himself. I received a satisfactory mark, not excellent, but it had been a compromise.

Toward the end of the course, we were video-taped doing practice teaching with our peers. I was the first candidate. Just as I was standing up to give my presentation, Frank U said, "Ken, you're stupid."

I was nervous enough without this ringing endorsement.

Another course was taught by two ordained ministers. I think it was part of a psychology course. It was very 'touchy-feely', warm and fuzzy. It was alien to a bunch of rough and tumble technicians, but I think we all needed it. We grudgingly enjoyed it.

Personally, I saw only saw one blatant act of racism at Queens. Joyce, our professor's assistant, knew the ropes, was a single mother, and was black. She was perfect to fill the professor's position when he retired.

However, they appointed a new person to take the position. Surprise! The replacement was white!

Graduation was coming. Peter's Paddle was a success. Part of its testing was to try to beat it against a cement wall. The paddle passed with flying colours. Its final test would come in real world conditions. We took the paddle to Portsmouth Harbour, just minutes from our college.

Peter said he'd give anyone a two-four of beer if they could master the kayak. He got one fool-hardy volunteer. Jamie was in the kayak for about fifteen seconds before it capsized. The paddle bobbed up, and passed the 'float' test. The water of Lake Ontario, near the St. Lawrence River, is frigid in early April. Guess what! No more takers.

I was looking forward to graduation until I found out that I couldn't wear the mortar-board graduation cap, with the tassel. It seemed strange to me; we were taking all the same basic courses as all the student teachers. Some snobby bureaucrat had decided that we would not receive a bachelor of education degree, and that we should be happy with an Ontario Teachers' Certificate. I was not a happy camper. The thinking was, and probably still is, that if you don't have a Bachelor of Arts (BA), --we said the BA stood for 'bugger-all' -- you couldn't receive a Bachelor of Education. I skipped graduation, and told them to mail the certificate to me!

Chapter Seventeen

Rookie Teacher Learns the Ropes

While my classmates were standing on the stage, with a few bureaucratic nincompoops, I was supply teaching. I spent six weeks in the Bracebridge High School. It sure boosted our standard of living. I rented a summer cabin in Bracebridge while there was still snow on the ground, convincing the owner to open it early, and not to worry about the amenities.

I was doing a great job of 'baching' it, especially once I discovered KFC (Kentucky Fried Chicken). I didn't have another home-cooked meal until my wife Margaret got there a couple weeks later.

Margaret was great but was having a tough time. She had just gone through a hysterectomy, and she needed a lot of recuperation time. Meanwhile, the darned dog had chewed up her dental bridge. Between the hysterectomy, and missing a bridge, she was devastated by the time she arrived at the cabin. She made friends with a chipmunk, and fed it out of her hand. This little interchange seemed to help a lot.

I introduced her to a young high school drop-out who was renting year- around, at the cabins. One night, he asked to talk to me in private. My poor wife thought I had something going on up there when I was 'baching' it. She confronted the drop-out.

"Anything you have to say to Ken, you can say in front of me," She told him.

The drop-out confessed that he simply wanted to know how to get rid of the crabs. We cracked up! He didn't think it was all that funny. After we finished laughing, we told him to retrieve the rest of his clothes, the majority of which he had tied in bundles in plastic bags, and submerged in our fast-running river. The crabs weren't going to be drowned!

I convinced him to go to the doctor and briefed him on blue ointment. Blue ointment was a standard air force treatment of crabs. (I forget his Christian name, since we just called him Crabs.)

We also remember Crabs for having fallen off a snowmobile, and being bitten by a rabid skunk. He had to get those painful needles in the belly. I couldn't make this stuff up if I tried!

My teaching stint ended two weeks before school was out. The staff monitored the exams, and wouldn't hire extra help, and thought their resident staff could handle it.

Teaching in Bracebridge was a valuable experience. I travelled the whole area, searching out Radio Shack stores, where I could buy electronic supplies. I sure wanted a full-time job in Bracebridge, but they only had an electrical position because their shop was fitted with electrical, not electronic, equipment. Wow. I found myself unemployed, without benefits to tie me over this time.

One Toronto newspaper carried all the want ads for most teaching positions in Canada. There seemed to be pages of them for other specialties.

My opportunities were limited to three positions; only one was for a high school teacher. That position was just listed as 'Perth County'. I knew the town of Perth was near Ottawa, and I would have applied to the North Pole to get a teaching job. The second position was at a community college with an opening for an electronics teacher, in Saskatchewan. The third, and that most interesting position, appeared to be in Liberia, Africa. I submitted my resume to all three institutions, and was accepted based on my credentials, depending on a final interview. I told the three recruiters that I would be taking the first firm position.

My first reply came from Perth County. It was a surprise to me that it was not near Ottawa at all, but actually twenty-five miles from Kitchener, in the town of Stratford which is the home to the world famous Stratford Festival. The town is small with population of about 25,000 people.

Before my final interview, we drove to Wildwood Lake, and stayed in a tent. The lake is actually a man-made reservoir, really beautiful in the summer, but not so nice in early May. We were really cold, as we only had blankets, no air mattresses, and slept on the tent floor. My daughter, my wife, and I, headed for MacDonald's Restaurant really early in the morning where I got cleaned up, and put on my interview suit. The interview went well, and they said they'd get back to me within the week.

The second reply came from a Saskatchewan community college. The school offered to provide a trip for me out West, to size up their community, before my final acceptance. The community college kept trying to entice me to accept their position.

One night, I got my resume out to see if I could have misrepresented myself in some way. It wasn't long after that, that I began to realize my value to them. I had passed the intensely difficult two-year electronic engineering course in only one year. This was exactly the curriculum I'd be teaching in Saskatchewan. Although many people had the technical knowledge, very few had inherent teaching skills. I had them both. My teaching certificate really paved the way, I think. I'm glad my future employers appreciated the importance of my credentials much more than I did.

The third position was in Liberia, Africa. It was populated by American slaves, who had been freed by James Munroe, then President of the U.S. On the face of it, freeing the slaves seems like a humane gesture, as he relocated them all to the new country of Liberia. It doesn't take much, in hindsight, to realize that he didn't want the freed blacks influencing the remaining millions of blacks still under slavery in the America.

If I took the job, I would be working for a consortium that was created between the Liberian government, and the giant Bethlehem Steel Corporation. I researched the country thoroughly. The government wanted a Liberian workforce trained in all aspects of the steel industry. I would be turning tribal class workers - their words, not mine – into electronics technicians.

While waiting for word back from Liberia, I went to a travel agent. She thought she was a comedienne, making a few cracks about shaking trees in Liberia to see what would fall out.

To say that my sixteen-year-old daughter was not keen on Liberia *before* was an understatement. But now, we had a real problem with Carol Ann. The agent stopped short of the word 'nigger', but just barely. This Zebra was NOT amused!

In the end, I decided to accept the offer from Perth County, and the next phase of my life was sheer joy. I was living my dreams due to my persistence, and hard work. (Successful dreams are results of action!) I still can't feel anything but satisfaction about my transition from a fifteen-year-old drop-out to a bonafide high school teacher. You, too, can do it!

I'll never forget the awe I felt when I walked under the huge marquee at Northwestern Secondary School. I remember saying to myself, "Who the hell do you think you are?" I so remember that going through my head! All of my schooling, and my twenty years of going nowhere in the military, had taken its toll on me. I was so unsure of myself, and felt so insecure about my new position. My saving grace was that I hid my apprehension completely. Having access to my classroom shop two weeks before school started really paid off. I was ready.

One day, I helped a young girl carry an armload of books into the school. I thought she must be helping her parents, but actually, she was a brand new teacher graduate just like me! The age difference sure stood out. She appreciated the fact that I thought she was a teenager.

We bonded as we were both brand new teachers. We played racquet sports together for five years. Mary was tall, and slim, and moved like a shot. I was older, heavier, and a lot slower than Mary was, but the power behind my shots ensured that many of the games we played were close.

She was the first university woman with whom I had ever played sports, so imagine my shock when she missed a return shot, and let loose with a series of amazing expletives which I hadn't heard since boot camp! So much for the pedestal I had placed her on. Some days, I'd come home, worn out. One time, when I collided with her racquet, I broke my glasses, and came home sporting a bloody nose. Margaret, asked, "What is she doing to you all day?"

I was given the position of the head of the sound, and lighting crew. Our department's job was to maintain all the spot lights, amplifiers and sound systems. The crew was made up of volunteer students from my electronics classes. It was a chance for them to gain real world experience. Even with my electronic/electrical knowledge, I had a lot to learn about stage lighting and the production of plays.

There always seemed to be a thin wall between technical, and academic, teachers. We blamed them, and they blamed us. I think they resented us because we only had to have a minimum of Grade Twelve. (They forgot the years of apprenticeships, and trade schools we had to endure.)

In all honesty, there were injustices on both sides. Tech teachers could get up to six years teaching experience on their salary grid based on their trade experience. Although most tech teachers started at pay level one, academic teachers started at pay level three. School boards had lots to learn.

Although I was teaching electronics, my community college courses were not reflected on my pay groupings. However, I started off in pay level group two. My Grade Thirteen courses were responsible for my higher group pay level. I accepted this pay jump regardless of the convoluted reasoning.

I decided to make an inquiry to the Teachers' College:

"What was the fastest way to a category four, not necessarily the easiest way?"

They spelled it out and were right on the money. Many technical teachers took academic courses to raise their pay level. I was forty-years-old to the day when I started teaching at Northwestern.

I knew a great technical teacher, who was a real gentleman. He started, and quit, those academic courses many times over. He said he couldn't see the relevance of the 'bird' courses (the simple general courses). He taught for twenty-five years and stayed in category one.

Being very mercenary, I realized there was a $10, 000 per year differential between group one, and group four pay. That really got my attention. As many pensions are based on the best five years of your salary, I had to play catch-up, as I'd started late.

I was given some well-meaning advice from many of my new-found colleagues, who had years of teaching experience. When you're on a two-year probationary teaching contract, the advice is: Work hard, volunteer to supervise extracurricular activities, and don't make waves until your contract becomes permanent.

I volunteered to be on our collective bargaining committee since I could finally voice my true opinions after having been so muzzled in the military. Our organization was much akin to a trade union, as we had the right to strike. We smugly called it a 'federation'. (Union sounded too militant to some of our so-called intellectuals who felt we shouldn't make waves, but bargain for our rights. That cracked me up!)

Being on the table committee of our collective bargaining unit was an eye-opener and not a pleasant experience for me. Our bosses, the principals and department heads, all belonged to the same negotiation team. The principals were management, big-time, and could progress no further as members of our federation. The only promotion a principal could get was to become a superintendent which would move them out of the bargaining group. This wasn't lost on me. I figured that many of our strategies were leaked to the school board bureaucrats, via these same principals. What a way to negotiate.

It looked like collusion to me, as far as our technical teachers were concerned. Our representatives would never have been party to this dialogue.

"Traditionally and historically, technical teachers have always taught one more period than academic teachers," I was told.

I was bowled over. What a bunch of crap. This requirement, that tech teachers had to teach one more period than academic teachers, had to be kept as a hush-hush arrangement – not written on paper. I lost it, and cursed at the management's side of the table. I made sure that no one was silencing me. I was removed from the table committee but was still on the team. Guess what! No more "traditionally and historically" nonsense. We were equal! It felt good.

As I said, I used to buy small electronic components from Radio Shack. Their part-time high school clerks tried to help customers but they had no experience, or electronics background. I convinced the manager that my senior students had both the knowledge, and the interest, to help boost his sales. He hired all 'student help' from that time forward on my recommendations. Years later, Greg, one of my senior students, managed that very same store.

One of my pet projects was a pinball machine. It was old, but it was also a lot of fun. The idea of "fun" did not go over well with the electrical teacher in the next room. He would have liked to see the old machine removed. The actual reason for using the pinball machine for teaching was an old technology called 'relay logic'. I would put faults in it, and let teams of two students troubleshoot, and fix it. The reward would be ten minutes of pinball. That wasn't in any teaching manual, but it sure was a great motivator. After two years, we couldn't get spare parts for the old machine, and we scrapped it. The poor machine suffered normal attrition.

I was aware that, if I picked up another technical teaching subject, down the road, it would count toward my category four pay level. I chose automotive studies which would qualify me to also teach Grades Nine and Ten auto mechanics. I felt comfortable in an auto shop as I had extensive experience rebuilding car engines with my stern old Pa. The next pay scale would offer more security and flexibility.

In the auto course, we had to strip old engines right down to the block. We then had to reassemble them, and they actually had to run after reassembly. It was just like I remembered when I was a kid. I had worked many hours alone on old engines when Dad was working. Up till then, I had forgotten the good times that the old car engines had provided to me.

The category four payscale was in my sights. It was called the Specialist Course. It could be taken in the summer at Althouse Teachers' College, a branch of Western University. The course was demanding, and tested our innovation skills. One large presentation was worth about 25 per cent of the marks.

My topic was: "Do teachers' strikes impede students, teachers, or both?" This was another chance to practise real free speech. In the service, you had to adhere to low-key rhetoric. I knew they had their reasons, but I wasn't in the air force now. So I decided to do a little acting. I made a picket sign, which depicted teachers as an uncaring, greedy bunch of money grubbers. (In real life, nothing could be further from the truth.)

We had many young teachers taking summer courses at Althouse. I accosted them with my one-man picket sign.

"How do you like being refused entry to school?" I said, trying to be very stern, grumpy and intimidating. "This is how your students feel when you set up picket lines to deny them their education!"

In reality, I had previously hidden the picket sign, in a bush, and had almost chickened out of accosting the student teachers, but in the end, I did pull it off. (They didn't gain access to the school.)

I was actually doing the stunt to stop my professor's car. When I saw his car, and I stopped him and I gave him a blurb that it was part of my introduction to my presentation. He liked it. I then scrammed, in a hurry, as I'm sure security had already been called. What a feeling it was to exercise my right of 'free speech'!

We worked hard, and played hard. There was a bar in London called Joe Cools. We hoisted a few pints there over the summer. One candidate had free run of his sister's fancy bungalow. She and her husband were touring all summer while we spent hours studying, barbequing and swimming in their full-size pool. Teaching did have its fringe benefits.

Chapter Eighteen

Seven Years - Commissioned Officer
Working with Army Cadets

We had our share of economically-deprived, poor kids, at my high school. Most of my students were boys. I noticed many of them were wearing parts of unidentifiable armed forces clothing - no flashes, Canada patches, badges or other insignia. The strange part was that they were all small sizes, and they fit the kids like they were tailored to them. The kids clued me in. They were part of the Cadet Corps, and they needed another army officer to help run the operation.

I kept mum about their supply of clothing. By regulation, it was only to be worn on cadet parade nights, and military functions. The kids also had good army boots. To hell with the book.

The Commanding Officer, George, was an ordained minister. He was also a hunter, a crack shot, and 'rough and tough'. He needed more manpower badly as he commuted from London to Stratford on cadet activities.

As teachers, we were not only youth-oriented but we were off all summer and much in demand to do a tour of summer camp.

The pay system was strange. The CO would get a 'lump sum' of money. This would be distributed, as fairly as possible, to our civilian instructors and officer staff. Ideally, our total would be a complement of eight people. I never saw a CO take one thin dime for wages.

We encouraged our staff to stay with the Cadet Corps. Sometimes, money talks, and so many of them stayed.

However, it was a long haul from my first interview until I became Commanding Officer of #223 Royal Canadian Army Cadet Corps.

George invited Margaret, and I, over to dinner in a high rise in London. I knew he would be 'feeling us out' as he said it was important for my wife to be onside, and be part of the team. The dinner went well and he was very generous with his wine. I thought it was part of the screening test, and limited myself to one small four-ounce glass. Marg didn't drink.

He flattered me, and it was good for my ego. I soon found out the facts of life. I had to go through the Basic Officers Qualifications (BOQ). Blimey! I had twenty years in the air force. Our Cadet Corps was affiliated with the Royal Canadian Regiment. It was real army infantry stuff.

If I would have reached the lofty rank of sergeant, I would have been exempt from the Basic Officers' Course. Because I was only a Master Corporal, I had to take many weekends of army training.

I kept silent about my twenty years in the air force. Most candidates had five years of army cadet training, and many also had army reserve training. Some had been regular army. The age of most of these young officer cadets would be about twenty-five years old.

I kept up, pretty well, on drill and marching. For many candidates, the army stuff was a refresher course, but it was all new to me. I had to learn map and compass, scurrying across pontoon and rope bridges, and all army stuff – for the first time. I probably appeared to be a little slow but, in reality, I was downright stubborn. No one in my platoon knew I had been a pigeon (air force). Upon graduation, when I spilled the beans, I earned some genuine respect.

The Army, Navy and Air Force Club in Stratford was our civilian sponsor. Most costs were covered by the Department of National Defence. Friday nights were a time for teachers to get together and unwind – until Army Cadets.

I was good with rifles. (Remember, I grew up in Dog Patch!) We had a rifle range in the basement of the Stratford Armoury. Party time was over. I devoted Friday nights to coaching target practice and to being the Range Safety Officer of our corps. It as an important responsibility; security, and safe use of weapons, were paramount. The next few years saw our Cadet Corps grow in both quality of training, and in numbers. We also had quite a few female cadets.

We managed to impose upon my wife, Margaret, to become a civilian instructor. She became our Supply Officer. We felt that, with more female staff, we would have fewer incidents with the young ladies of our corps, plus they would have a female staff member nearby to confide in, if they needed.

One young lady was particularly hard to handle. Unbeknownst to her, I had recruited her mother as part of our staff. The daughter almost quit, but we were glad she didn't. It worked. She was well behaved after that, and she flourished, and realized her potential.

The basic course for Officers' Training was taught at CFB Borden. I was well organized, and gave practice lectures. I was a driven man. Even though I was now teaching, I was also in the Reserve Army. I was going to get my Queen's Commission in Canada's Armed Forces come hell or high water. This is the same Commission earned by any other officer in any field of the Armed Forces. How an 'over-forty' ex-airman could keep up with the physical side of drill, and marching, was a test of my determination. I had superb marks except for drill. In drill, they said I was average. Personally, I think they were generous on the 'average' mark.

Every weekend, I would head up to Borden from our home in Stratford for the entire summer.

Our Senior NCOs were a pretty good bunch. They knew they would be saluting us and calling us 'Sir' upon graduation!

Summer camp for training the Cadets was very demanding for some of us. It depended on what job you had. One guy was paid Captain's pay to teach the cadets how to fish! Some poor kids had never seen the woods, much less a fishing line. (Just remember that some were inner city kids.)

The pay was extraordinary. I was still getting my annual teacher's salary plus captain's pay for two months in the summer. What a bonanza.

Some of us were in constant contact with our platoon of students. I think I had two days off in two months. Official Cadet Training would cease on Friday afternoons, and we then had to amuse, entertain, and mother all the kids who couldn't go home on the weekends. In our spare time we were expected to attend the sports leagues, corn boils, and be readily available for any emergency which could happen among a with kids.

Companies were made up of about a hundred kids each, and we had at least five companies! It was very satisfying to see these kids mature, and grow up, over a summer. With this huge responsibility to the Cadets and their parents, I made sure that I never had an alcoholic drink for the duration of summer camp.

There was always some animosity between our supply source at CFB London's Woolsey Barracks, and our part-time CIL (Cadet Instructors List) Officers. The regular force supply group would only deliver our trucks full of tents, sleeping bags, and all other camping gear during the day. This was a problem because all our officers all had full-time jobs. It would have been helpful if they could have delivered after five o'clock, but the supply sergeants were adamant. It was time for me to make another attitude adjustment, and get innovative.

I had the Woolsey Barracks supply truck deliver the equipment to the back door of my shop class at school. They would back the army truck up, and my cadets would make short work the unloading them. We would store the loot in my shop for quick distribution to our exercise/operations field just before the weekend of camping was to begin. A few non-cadets didn't like the smell of moth balls, and canvas, but my exploits were never reported to the Principal's Office.

Everyone assumed I had twenty years in the army, and I hadn't told them differently. I was unwilling to disclose my air force background because some old army types would have given me the gears.

Historically, there was always friction between the army, air force and navy personnel, and this was ARMY Reserves. I must have looked pretty thick on my army routines, tasks and skills. Necessity forced me to become a quick learner. Fortunately, supervising a platoon of kids was more or less crowd control unless they were marching.

One day, the expert canoe instructor was demonstrating proper canoeing. The first order of business was to teach safety, in case the canoe inadvertently capsized. I had been in a canoe only once - one of my many secrets. Another secret was that I really didn't know how to swim. I could float, but swim? No! Apparently, those in the army learned to swim well at boot camp, but it wasn't part of the course for air force 'pigeons'. The instructor 'joe'd' me into showing the technique of hanging onto the canoe when it capsized. I wasn't sure about the technique but I knew I would have no trouble hanging on to the canoe. Even when I put the life jacket on, I found out that FEAR is a great motivator.

I was scared to death!

Somehow, I got to the middle of the piddly little lake. Just before the instructor blew the whistle – that was my call to action to upset the canoe -- lightning hit! Apparently, we weren't allowed on the water in a lightning storm -- whistle be damned!

The instructor bellowed at me, "Get that canoe ashore 'tout de suite'.

I accomplished that maneuver in a jiffy, before he changed his mind. My secrets were safe. I never again pulled canoeing duty at summer camp.

The only other mind-boggling event, that summer, was called rappelling. To the uninitiated, it meant simply jumping off a thirty-seven foot tower using two ropes – one to guide us, and the other to put friction on the 'brake rope' to slow us down. My cadets had previously received extensive instruction in rappelling techniques. I had NONE!

I was in charge of marching them to the tower, and controlling them, while each one took a turn. The rappelling training program paid off beautifully for our cadets. There was not one slip-up or incident; I was proud of my kids.

That's when the bubble burst! The rappel master was a regular army rappelling expert. He spotted me and yelled out, "Sir, would you like to have a go?" I knew my fifteen- and sixteen-year-old cadets had all rappelled successfully. I really had no choice. I said, "Sure Corporal, I'll be right up."

Panic Stations! I ran up the steep stairs, about the equivalent of a four-storey building, hustling up before I lost my nerve. I tried to figure the ropes out during my run to the top.

Let's be clear: I knew I was in no physical danger as they had lots of safeguards but I was deadly afraid of being embarrassed. If I exited wrongly, I could be going down head first before they stopped me. Somehow, I did the perfect exit and rappelled down. At least, that's what it looked like to the people on the ground. In reality, the leather glove on my guide hand was smoking. I was trying to use the guide rope as the brake rope. How would I know? I had never seen rappelling before, or since. Remember, the kids had experienced hours of expert instruction. I had zilch!

I got to the bottom. No one knew my glove was smoking, and my hand was blistering. Ah! Success! The kids were clapping. The Master Corporal said, "You did good, sir. Would you like to try it again?"

He had to be kidding!

I said, "I'd love to, Corp, but I have to get these kids to the mess hall." Never again without any lessons!

The CO of our Stratford Cadet Corps was leaving. The army thought I didn't have enough experience to run a corps. At that point, they were probably right. We ended up with a Major as our CO. He had been a cadet, and rose through the Cadet Instructors List, but he had no reserve, or regular army experience. He seemed to me to be a 'prima donna'.

The only one he got along with was my wife, who had a misplaced admiration for him. As our Supply Officer, who was really new to the whole army concept, she depended on him for guidance and advice.

We were turning in bedsheets, after an exercise, and we were short about half a dozen. Marg knew the long drawn out procedures to get them written off. Someone's head would probably roll, or a pay deduction would be made, to cover the shortage. I showed her how to make the tally equal to the total sheets signed out. It was simple. Rip the sheets in two, and fold them. If I wasn't her husband, I knew she would have sung to the Major. She was honest to a fault, and shocked that I could be so 'resourceful'. She was not impressed!

The Major had a house trailer at Ipperwash which I could use while at summer camp. It was so close to the base that I could sleep off-camp. He promised us that accommodation. At least I would see my wife because she could come with me. Of course, I volunteered for summer camp. Just before I departed, he said he changed his mind and said that he was going to use the trailer all summer. That was a bummer.

One day I was Orderly Officer. Some cadets got hold of me, and said there was a drunken Officer Cadet harassing them in the barracks. These quarters are strictly out-of-bounds except for duty staff. I was marching down to see him when a staff car pulled up beside me. It was one of our camp padres with a couple of guests. He carried the rank of Major.

I said I would like to chat but had this pressing problem to sort out. He asked, "What are you going to do?"

I told him the truth.

"I'm going to take that Officer Cadet to jail in the guardhouse. The Major intervened, promising that Officer Cadet would remain in his custody, and that he would be responsible for him overnight. I told him I still had the responsibility to report it, which I did. I never saw the Officer Cadet again. I think he was asked to resign.

Having served twenty years in the military, I knew all about inventories. When you take over an inventory account, you have to count everything. I was taking it over from a reserve sergeant who was in a big, big hurry for me to accept the inventory.

No way. I counted everything. Everything was there. He was miffed that it took so long but it was my responsibility, and he had to live with the delay. I had heard of several cases where the new officers did a cursory check and signed for everything. Later on, they found out they had signed for a bunch of wood pallets that the reserve NCOs were using the wood to build small patios for the camping trailers in the staff trailer camp. I'm sure they must have gotten the pallets written off, but they were much wiser inventory holders after that.

Back at my day job, there was always some fluctuating enrollment in optional subjects like the technical trades. If it looked like there might be declining enrollment, the principal had to give you written notice about a half-time position.

I was the only teacher qualified for the Assistant Head job for our department. One teacher had spent years at a lower category, and never completed the courses until this opening was coming available. I said I didn't mind half-time; it was the half-pay I didn't like. They assured me it was a necessary formality, which it was, and that I should not be worried.

Jim was a real nice guy. After his course, both he and I would be applying for the promotion. He and the Technical Director had been at the school together forever.

Ma didn't raise a fool. I applied at Waterloo County Board of Education. Our counties shared the county line. They paid better but I would have happily stayed in Stratford because, by then, I had bought, renovated, and sold four houses.

Rappelling with no lessons? Zowwweeeeeeee! Cadets from 1982 to 1987 really changed lives for the young cadets.

Promoted to Captain in the Army Reserves. Happy Days 1984-1987

ANAF Sponsor / Representative with Capt. McKnight
and award-winning Army Cadet 1984-87

Chapter Nineteen

My Nightmares as a Landlord

I was in the landlord business big time, for me. One of my houses was an old side-by-side duplex located in Mitchell about twelve miles west of Stratford. I had to buy both sides, as it was all built on one lot, and only one owner was allowed.

It was necessary to up-grade the electrical system to one hundred ampere service on each side. I had no problem assisting Barry, the electrician. The job went well, without a hitch, until we had to feed the larger power-wires into the mast. My electrician suddenly informed me that he was afraid of heights. I ended up standing on the roof, feeding the wires down the mast pipe. These were large wires that we covered with silicone to make them very slippery. I completed the job without breaking my neck. Happily, I had no problems with the electrical inspector since all the work was signed by my licensed electrician.

I was shopping for new insurance on the duplex. My insurance lady, who lived in Goderich, looked at the address, and couldn't believe her eyes. She had lived in that very same house twenty-five years ago. Now, the bad news. She wouldn't insure it without some fire safety modifications which should have been carried out twenty-five years earlier. Needless to say, the improvements were done, and the insurance was put in place.

What I really needed was insurance against bad tenants.

One jerk tenant gave me a rubber cheque - NSF. He wouldn't come to the door no matter what. I was infuriated. Because I had helped with the electrical work, I knew a very important fact. My daughter, as a tenant, lived in the other side of the house. 'Jerk tenant's' main fuse box was on my daughter's side of the primitive basement. Without telling her what I was doing, I delighted in pulling the switch, and leaving him in the dark.

I was feeling really proud of myself as I cruised down the highway to Stratford. An OPP lit me up. I stopped. We stood in front of his headlights. Boy, did I get an earful. He said that I had caused some trouble for one of my tenants and that the tenant said his lights were out.

"Gee I'm sorry," I said. "I was doing work in my daughter's basement, and must have shut the box off by mistake."

Then, I continued, and dug out the rubber cheque.

"Isn't this against the law?" I asked. "I thought an NSF cheque was fraud, theft or obtaining goods or services falsely."

"I'll give you half an hour to restore his power," the cop said, looking at the cheque. "When I check to see if his power is on, I will have a very frank talk with him about issuing bad cheques."

I returned to the duplex immediately, and the tenant got his power back. Personally, I thought the officer was unimpressed. Carol Ann was really not amused when I told her I had shut her friend's power off without telling her, and that I got pulled over by the cops. She kind of smirked. Her poor father had been through a rough night, and all she was worried about was her girlfriend next door. Long story short, I got the money and they moved.

There was the usual upkeep and headaches that come with being a landlord and then, there was the unexpected.

An old septic system collapsed beside the new tenant's picnic table. I was dumbfounded! We were on town water! The town was supposed to have removed the tank years ago. I quickly rented a tractor, with a bucket, as I was worried about the tenant's nice little kids tumbling into the abyss. Five hundred dollars later, the hole was filled in, and I then had some piece of mind.

I had lots of loose ends to tidy up before accepting the Cambridge teaching position. We were enjoying our newly purchased semi-detached home in Cambridge – all to ourselves! No tenants! I sold the semi-detached property in Mitchell, and got rid of the tenants. Next, I converted the large bungalow in Stratford, into a triplex, failing to apply for building permits. I figured forgiveness was easier than getting permission. I was dead wrong. One of my new tenants, in this triplex, had a beef with another one of the tenants. He reported to the Fire Department that the other tenant had a propane tank in his kitchen which was not true.

It was totally wrong but the damage had been done. The Fire Chief arrived and then, called the building inspector. The building inspector had no sense of Ha Ha. He threw a fit. I was marking time in front of him, and the Fire Chief! Many thousands of dollars later, the Stratford project was once again a large single bungalow. It now had two kitchens and five bedrooms. (Don't tell anybody, but the third kitchen's plumbing was now buried behind new gyproc!)

Carol Ann, my daughter, had become a landlord owning a semi-detached (both sides) and she ran into her own share of bad landlord experiences. After a series of landlord hassles, combined with a run of bad luck that seems to follow her, Carol Ann and her three kids moved in with us in Cambridge.

Marg got a job cleaning hotel rooms. I used to walk her to the bus stop right beside Winston Churchill Park. Her 6:50 a.m. bus was always on time. I waved to Marg every morning, once she was on the bus, and the bus driver always waved back. I was beginning to wonder if he thought I was sweet on him! Ha-ha! Marg and I had some good laughs over this experience.

My school was next to the Winston Churchill Park, and being a doting grandfather, I took the three urchins (grand-kids) to the park. They were still young, perhaps eight, five and three. I told them, in my firm teacher's voice, "Stick together!" Naturally, they scattered in three different directions.

Richard, the oldest, climbed into a tall rocket-ship, which was part of the playground equipment. He got scared, and was hesitant to come down. My bellowing voice probably didn't help the situation. When I think back, now, I realize that it was no wonder he didn't come down. Like a cat, the louder you yell, the farther up the tree they climb! I had visions of the fire department having to come and cut him out.

Can you imagine the local headlines news?

Local teacher's grandson had to be rescued by fire department.

When asked why he wouldn't come down, he would say, "Grandfather kept yelling at me!"

Geez, I was in sheer panic mode! I have a loud voice even when I'm not yelling. I vowed, that day, if I ever got him out of that rocket-ship, that I wasn't taking these 'turds' to the park ever again.

A young woman, who was very small of stature, saw my dilemma. She was able to fit right into the rocket, and she coaxed Richard back to the ground.

I kept my promise. Never again did I take 'them turds' to the park. (Liz, the little one, had a slight speech impediment, and said, "Grandpa, we aren't toids!")

Chapter Twenty

Racism Comes to a Boiling Point - Championing Diversity

Summer was over, and I stepped into my new position, teaching in Cambridge, at Glenview Park Secondary School. I fit in with the new staff right from the beginning. We shared Friday nights at the Legion, enjoying a feeling of real comradeship. Four, or five of us, would also have lunch together.

Then it started. Before this upcoming incident, I thought I was being overly sensitive about racial remarks I had heard. Maybe I was looking too hard for them. One guy, our leader, started with the 'N' jokes. Most guys laughed politely. One younger teacher, who I was trying to mentor, had no expression. No wonder, because it was our boss who was telling the joke – a lousy one at that; it was totally in bad taste.

I lost it! I pounded on the table so hard I thought it would split. All my buried anger, and emotions, came rushing out. I almost grabbed him. I was half-crying, and totally screaming at him. The joke teller could see his career, and pension, disappearing. He went pale. Friday couldn't come soon enough.

Later on, one teacher on hall duty asked, "What happened down there, Ken? It looked like World War III was about to start."

Another teacher, who had never joined us at the Legion before, came and sat with us. I was suspicious that he was a spy looking for fallout from the racist comment incident. The last person you need is a racist pig. I blatantly told him I was on to him, and that he could go right back and report to his boss!

I was still really upset, and angry, as I relayed the story to my wife that evening. I was going to do nothing about the boss' racist 'jokes', but if TV cameras would start following us down the school halls, he would know that he had cheesed off the wrong lady.

My wife, Marg, really wanted to blow the whistle but she didn't, and the cameras never came.

I ate alone in my classroom after that. The culprit visited me, and said he was fond of me. He said that he liked telling jokes, and that he wasn't racist.

"Jokes are funny," I explained. "But your version of jokes are way less than funny."

I had tried so hard to become a successful teacher and was determined to put that racial incident behind me.

Until one day.

It seems all my heroes have feet of clay. This guy never got it. One day he told me, "You should have told us you were black. I would never have joked about it."

Yeah, right!

One day, he had a guest; I think he was a reeve of a township. When that guest came over to me, I shook his hand.

"Hi, I am Ken McKnight," I said, adding, "I'm black."

Then, I walked away, leaving behind a very confused public official.

I expect that the racist must have had some explaining to do. Yup! That cleared the air. No more black jokes!

A bit later, the young teacher I was mentoring came up to me.

"I am so ashamed that I did nothing," he said. "My Dad's a religious man, and if he knew I had said nothing to protect you, he would have been so disappointed in this son's inaction."

I assured him that he had done nothing wrong.

I was upwardly mobile. I wanted to retire after twenty years of teaching, so it was in my best interest to pursue the position of Assistant Director of Technical Education. The only snag was that it probably meant relocating yet again. As you probably know, most pensions are based on your best five years of income. With only twenty, not twenty-five or thirty years in, as was the norm, I felt that increasing my salary was paramount.

I got my break, and was appointed Assistant Technical Director at Waterloo-Oxford High School. I knew this was my last promotion as I was retiring in about three years. It was a new start.

I thought that the staff and students would be less likely to judge people because of religion, race or origin. We had a large cross-section of people of German descent. Many of them remembered stories about their great grandparents from World War I, and stories from grandparents remembering the Holocaust from World War II who often experienced first hand, and for decades, the stigma of being German. (During World War I, a town in Southwestern, Ontario changed its name from Berlin to Kitchener.)

We had about fourteen hundred students in our school. Virtually all were bussed as we served parts of three counties, which meant we also had lots of farm kids. We had exciting, and meaningful, noon hour activities and sports. Our girls' field hockey team was a robust bunch. I think every other school was intimidated by their fitness and their will to win.

We were a very large rural campus which was measured in acres. After a few attempts to actively patrol the grounds, we had to settle for this plan.

The students had a lookout at the top of the hill, and students would be alerted, with a shrill whistle, when a duty teacher was spotted.

Cigarettes disappeared, clothing was rearranged, and the little angels immediately started studying or just shooting the breeze. Nobody fooled anyone, but at least this constant patrolling kept most problems under control.

The trouble was that we had to catch the little offenders to discipline them. It wasn't easy, when all you saw was a group of well-mannered kids. I guess they knew we cared about them since many treated it more like a game; they were pretty mature to put up with the invasion of 'their space'.

I coached the junior soccer teams. I had no coaching experience but believed in honesty and sportsmanship, and I told the kids this is what I expected. The simple fact was, I was the only teacher who would fill the position. We had so many clubs, and sports, that many teachers were already helping with two activities. It was kind of neat that we had such vigorous noon hour and after school programs.

Professional Development Days are designed to broaden our overall teaching knowledge. I know some parents resent them because it is a challenge for them to get childcare. Parents are trying to hold down sometimes two jobs to eek out a living, and P.D. Days just add to their stress level.

Thankfully, the majority of Canadian parents still respect our profession so, although they may resent the inconvenience, they don't give teachers much flak. Experience tells me that if you tell most Americans you are a teacher, the results are less than flattering. Some think that's the only job you can do, and others feel sorry for you. When you see the crummy wages they pay teachers in the some of the United States, coupled with the minimum education required in parts of the United States, their attitudes are understandable.

Wouldn't you know it? My last Grade Nine class was the 'class from Hell'! Twenty years of meaningful teaching and I was stuck with these 'darlings'.

Their reputation had preceded them. I pulled their student files in preparation, as I did with all my classes. Many seemed incorrigible. Waiting for them in the hallway on the first day of class, I held the door open and casually said, "Sit where you want fellows, we're going to have a good semester."

I could see the sneering looks, the eyes darting from one kid to the other and I overheard one kid say, "We've got a live one. It's going to be a blast!"

"Is everyone comfortable?" I asked.

"Sure, Teach", the ringleader responded.

My demeanor changed instantly. I put on my best scowl, and I growled, and ordered all the guys in the back seats to change places with the guys in the front.

"Pronto! Schnell!"

(It doesn't hurt to have them think you're a little bit crazy. It keeps them off balance.)

Uncharacteristically, the urchins obeyed. I remembered that I had been a rebellious student myself and we had all headed for the back rows in those days. Nothing has changed.

The next challenge was the constant complaining.

"We want a field trip."

They were getting my goat. I finally leveled with them.

"I wouldn't take you guys across the road, much less on a field trip!" I told them.

One day, their established leader started again with, "We want a field trip."

"Okay," I said.

He was proud, and was darned near speechless for over a minute. Again, I saw the knowing looks from one to the other.

"Where are we going?" he asked.

"Do you really care?" I retorted. "You will be out of the classroom all afternoon."

"That's right Teach," leader said. "I don't care where we go, but when are we going?"

"Right now," I said, "It's all set up and ready to go."

There were a lot of school yard lawyers in this class.

"How about permission slips?" they asked.

"I'll take responsibility for them."

I could see by their demeanor what was coming next. They were already spending the money from their future lawsuits. The students, and I, all knew that parental consent forms must be filled in for any off-campus event. They were just waiting to sue me, and the school board, at the drop of a hat.

"Let's go," I said.

They gleefully trooped out toward the buses.

Then I barked, "I told you I would never cross the street with you guys!"

Their headman figured it out. We could cut across the campus sports field, target the buses and never cross the street.

Bright boy.

They got into the middle of our enormous sports field. I again called for them to halt. They were perplexed. Again, it didn't hurt for them to think I was a little crazy.

"This is a field, right?" I said to the fearless leader.

"Yeah, I guess," he answered.

"You guessed right. This is your field trip, 'capiche'?"

I'm not as callous as sometimes I appear. I had arranged for our class to watch a rocket firing display, created and demonstrated, by another class. Even the tough kids were amazed.

Whoosh! Whoosh! Whoosh! Up went the rockets, one after another - twenty-four to be exact. Each kid had built one and we watched them disappearing into the bright sunlight, and blue sky.

"How do you like the rockets?" I asked. They were thrilled.

"How would you like to build them and launch them yourselves?" I asked. "One condition: no more 'tough guy' bull and no more malarkey. We will be working with gunpowder, which is extremely dangerous, so therefore you MUST follow my orders. Safety is paramount."

That was the end of the tough guy scenarios. It proved to me that there is good in most kids. Sometimes you have to throw away the psychology books and become a totally free thinker, with non-traditional ideas.

I had attended more than my share of military funerals in my younger years, while I was a member of a one hundred man honour guard. We had many young pilots who were killed flying the new 104 jets and other military aircraft. Our Honour Guard also stood and remembered the fallen personnel of many other military tragedies.

Remembrance Day was a big part of my life. The first year, at my new school, they decided not to hold a Remembrance Day ceremony. I thought fleetingly that it might be because of the many people of Germanic background. But that made no sense at all. Many of these parents had lost loved ones and suffered, too. It must have been an oversight, I thought, and that's when I raised proper hell.

The vice-principal's solution was to arrange to have my classes covered so that I could go to the ceremony. I blew up!

"It's not for me," I said. "It's for the kids! I remember the sacrifices. The ceremony I'm expecting here at the school is for the new generations of students!"

The next year we had a ceremony. The woman who organized it had one message: War is evil. War must be banned.

We all knew that. She had totally missed the point, that our young men, and women, had experienced great self-sacrifice and had been buried in the ground in the prime of their lives.

The next year, it was as it should be. We even had World War II veterans give us a somber talk. The message got through.

I had decided I would follow through with my long range plan. I've always said that I have -- or had – twenty-twenty vision. I had *twenty* years in the air force followed by my electronic engineering technician course. Then I spent my year at Queens' University Teachers' College. Then I spent *twenty* years teaching.

You see? Twenty-twenty!

The excitement of climbing the ladder of success waned. I was no longer driven to compete for promotions in the teaching profession.

Time for more travel with wife Marg. Visiting Northern B.C.

Chapter Twenty-One

Retirement - The Canadian Dream

Marg and I began living the Canadian Dream. We had a lovely mobile home on top of the cliff facing Lake Huron. Every day was a delight. They don't call it Blue Water Country for nothing. I could walk trails, and interrupt deer and other small animals, at my leisure.

I counted maybe twenty-one deer in the field one evening. It was beautiful. We knew full well what the winters would be like. Call it Lake Effect Country, Squall Country, or White Country if you will, but understand that even in good weather, there are no buses, trains, airplanes or boats out of there. Our planned solution was to become snowbirds, wintering from November to April in Florida.

We rented a place on Saddlebag Lake near Lake Wales, Florida. We tried it out, and decided to buy in the same community the following year. We bought from a real honest Canadian Snowbird whose wife was ill; he had to reduce his rental holdings. This was a reminder, for me, about just how fragile our Snowbird years might be. We had thirteen years to enjoy our winter paradise in Florida before Marg's medical challenges brought us back to full-time retirement in Canada.

Paradise Lost – Our Vacation Home in Florida was flooded circa 2009

While we were down there, I ran into the worst racist I have had the misfortune of knowing. Before we settled into our final mobile purchase, we met a fellow with a place for sale who offered to take me fishing in his pontoon boat.

The trip was actually about one-tenth fishing, and nine-tenths hard selling. He thought the one optimum selling point was this: "We only have one nigger in our gated community."

He smiled through his rotten teeth and continued, "Yeah, and we own him."

Can you believe it? The man who said this to me was a Canuck. Yes, that's right my fellow countrymen, he was a Canadian!

The black man he was referring to worked in our gated community, and was a perfect gentleman at all times, no matter what he had to put up with.

Needless I immediately came to the black man's defence! I railed at this fool who stood in front of me, but nothing registered with him. My words went right over his racist head.

It turns out, that 'cracker' fool had a reputation of being a 'wheeler-dealer'. Most Canadians avoided him. He, and his red-necked bigoted friends, held court every week; they sat around playing poker, and trying to relive the American Civil War. As far as I'm concerned, they deserved each other. Let's not forget who won the 'war of the States'. The Southern Slavers lost to the Northern Free States!

One American friend of mine was ambivalent about racism, to my face, anyway. He was the only one who I knew who beat the 'wheeler-dealer' at buying or selling.

Clay, in good conscience, sold that racist a golf cart. The guy bargained the price down and was very vocal about how clever he was to get such a good deal. The cart fell apart. The only tears that were shed were those of our 'wheeler-dealer'.

Clay always travelled first-class. He sent me to his high-class barber. I really couldn't afford him but Clay was persuasive. Thank goodness that I still looked white. This barber was 100 per cent KKK. I kept my mouth shut because he had a razor in his hand.

These encounters with such simpletons were the only blemish in paradise.

During our time in Florida, we picked sweet oranges from our orange tree for breakfast. The American gas and food prices were also easy to take as were the country music concerts, sunshine, and no snow to shovel.

After twelve glorious years, we realized paradise comes at a cost. During year thirteen, Marg's medical situation dictated that we enjoy a shorter southern stay than we had planned for. We had pretty good health coverage but were uneasy about what a long hospital stay would cost down south.

Our last winter in Saddlebag Park was interrupted by four returns to Canada to deal with Marg's medical issues. That was the end for us in Florida. We moved back to a house that we still owned in Stratford. It had been rented out and required some renovations. I was a better carpenter's helper than I was a carpenter, so I hired capable handymen and helped them, thus reducing my overhead.

There are no friends like old friends. That's a quote by a very wise but unknown author. We had kept in touch with a particular couple over the decades – since the girls' underwear had been hanging on the screen doors! Marg, and her friend, had worked at the hospital in Middleton, Nova Scotia, when they were both sixteen. These friends now lived in

Trenton, Ontario after they had retired from CFB Trenton. (Just as a point of interest, Trenton is now known as Quinte West.)

My granddaughter was getting married in Picton in Prince Edward County outside of Belleville. During our stay in Belleville to attend the wedding, we fell in love all over again with the Quinte area. It felt like we had come home.

I listed our house and it took one year to sell. I guess my stubborn streak was still in place because I got my price by waiting. We moved to the Quinte area, re-uniting with our lifelong friends.

I'm a member of two service clubs: the Army-Navy-Air Force Club, and the Canadian Legion. Most recently, I joined the Belleville Speak-Easy Toastmasters Club, a branch of Toastmasters International.

After a night of cooking for the Legion members, we were sitting around discussing food preparation and health inspectors. One of the guys had a problem with a health inspector. Why? The health inspector wasn't white! The fellow said to us, his captive audience, "He's not like us, if you know what I mean."

Another member responded, "No, I don't know what you mean."

"You know....., he's different," the racist continued.

"Do you mean he's not white?" asked another.

Our racist replied calmly, "Yep, I guess that IS what I'm saying." Amazing how nothing much had changed. Yet again, I hear the change after all, where the other members called him on it. There's hope for us yet!

I am sitting on our eighth floor balcony here, in Belleville. The view of the Bay of Quinte is magnificent. Our apartment has access to an indoor swimming pool, sauna and a park-like setting complete with BBQs and picnic tables.

It makes you wonder how far I could have gone if I was white. That sentence was meant as a joke! I've finally figured things out. It's what you are, and who you are, in character that makes the difference. It's not your roots. You have no control over your hereditary background.

After reaching this crusty curmudgeonly age of seventy-five years, this is my learned reaction. You can't help what the idiots, and racists, think. It's positive action that counts. Do good things, anyway!

This final chapter in my book -- hopefully not the final chapter in my life -- has been hard to lay down in print. I felt a bit of sadness, and melancholy, tried to creep in during the writing of my story.

I must apologize for a lack of humour in some chapters of my book because when I was writing, some very vivid flashbacks appeared before my eyes. Some were not funny, but I wanted to be truthful.

Putting up with, and overcoming racism, has given me the guts to look to the future, and beyond. Closing in on seventy-six years, I have to recognize my own mortality. What a ride! It's been worth it!

P.S.: Oh, by the way, I'm still a Canadian Zebra. However, I am no longer one *Angry* Canadian Zebra! I now embrace the word *Zebra* -- and celebrate life!

Recommended Reading

'The Children of Africville' by Christine Welldon
Nimbus Publishing
Nimbus.ca

About The Author

Ken McKnight was born in 1939 at the end of the Great Depression. He graduated from the 'school of hard knocks'. Due to economic necessity, he became a 15 year old high school drop-out. Ken was born into an interracial mulatto / white family but could and did pass for white. Why not? The author inadvertently discovered his bi-racial background as a preteenager. His family never acknowledged his bi-racial origin. This secret, and the white environment in which he lived, subjected him to an onslaught of racial slurs from bigots who thought he was as white as them. He first heard the word 'Zebra' used to describe a bi-racial person when 22 years old. His first reaction was shock! Today he embraces and celebrates the word 'Zebra'. Although not the only defining factor in his life, the racial slurs gave him grit and determination to succeed in the white man's world - and succeed he did! Night school, summer school and correspondence courses were completed while doing a full-time 20 year stint in the Royal Canadian Air Force. Ken earned the two-year Electronic Engineering Technician Certificate from Loyalist College, Belleville, ON. Following this, he attended the Faculty of Education at Queen's University, Kingston, ON earning his Ontario Teaching Certificate. Ken successfully taught high school electronics and retired after 20 enjoyable, memorable years. His motto: "Don't ever give up!" Viva la Zebra!

Printed in Canada